THE HOME UNIVERSITY LIBRARY
OF MODERN KNOWLEDGE

200

ARCHITECTURE

F. J. Broadbent.

Architecture

MARTIN S. BRIGGS
F.R.I.B.A.

Illustrated by the Author

Geoffrey Cumberlege
OXFORD UNIVERSITY PRESS
LONDON   NEW YORK   TORONTO
1947

PRINTED IN GREAT BRITAIN
3646

CONTENTS

1. WHAT IS ARCHITECTURE?   1

2. THE BEGINNINGS   6

3. THE GREEKS   18

4. THE ROMANS   32

5. THE DARK AGES   48

6. NORMAN ARCHITECTURE   67

7. EARLY GOTHIC ARCHITECTURE IN ENGLAND
   (c. 1150–1350)   85

8. LATE GOTHIC ARCHITECTURE IN ENGLAND
   (c. 1350–1550)   106

9. THE DAWN OF THE RENAISSANCE IN ENGLISH
   ARCHITECTURE (c. 1550–1620)   122

10. INIGO JONES AND CHRISTOPHER WREN
    (1620–1714)   140

11. LATE RENAISSANCE ARCHITECTURE IN ENG-
    LAND (1714–1820)   156

12. 'THE BATTLE OF THE STYLES' (1820–1900)   169

13. TWENTIETH-CENTURY ARCHITECTURE IN
    ENGLAND (1900–1939)   185

14. ARCHITECTURE IN NORTH AMERICA SINCE
    1620   200

BIBLIOGRAPHY   215

INDEX   219

LIST OF ILLUSTRATIONS

1. Primitive Building: A, Lewis, N.B.; B, Scrivelsby, Lincs.; C, Dymock, Glos.   7
2. Portico of Mehenkwetre's House, *c.* 2000 B.C. (from a model in his tomb).   7
3. South Temple at Thebes: Sectional view (after Choisy).   13
4. Façade of the Shrine of Anubis at Deir el-Bahari   13
5. The Temple of Hephaistos (or 'Theseion') at Athens: View as at present.   21
6. The Temple of Hephaistos (or 'Theseion') at Athens: Plan.   21
7. The Choragic Monument of Lysikrates at Athens (restored).   21
8. The Greek and Roman Orders.   24
9. The Roman Aqueduct ('Pont du Gard') near Nîmes.   39
10. The Roman Temple ('Maison Carrée') at Nîmes.   39
11. The Pantheon, Rome: Interior.   41
12. Baths of Diocletian, Rome: Central Hall (now church of S. Maria degli Angeli).   41
13. The Arch of Constantine, Rome.   45
14. Flats and Shops at Ostia near Rome (restored).   45
15. Basilican Church of S. Sabina, Rome: Interior.   52
16. Parenzo: Atrium of the Cathedral.   54
17. Mosque of Ibn Tūlūn, Cairo: Arcade in Sanctuary.   57
18. Church of St. Lawrence, Bradford-on-Avon.   65
19. Earl's Barton Church, Northamptonshire.   66
20. Iffley Church, near Oxford.   73
21. Kilpeck Church, Herefordshire: Doorway   75
22. Diagrams of Vaulting.   77

vi

23. A typical Norman Cathedral: Sectional View and Plan. 80

24. Salisbury Cathedral: (a) View from N.W.; (b) Ground Plan. 90

25. Salisbury Cathedral: Sectional View. 97

26A. Early-Gothic Capital: Lincoln. 99

26B. Mid-Gothic Capital: Southwell. 99

27. Winchelsea Church: East end 100

28. Gothic Windows and Doorways. 101

29. King's College Chapel, Cambridge: Sectional View. 109

30. Stokesay Castle, Shropshire. 109

31. Penshurst Place, Kent: The Great Hall. 114

32. Henry VII's Tomb, Westminster Abbey. 126

33. Aston Hall, Birmingham: (a) Air-view, c. 1620; (b) Ground Plan. 130

34. A Yorkshire Stone House: Guiseley Rectory. 133

35. Cotswold Stone Cottages at Bibury, Gloucestershire. 133

36. The 'Old House', Hereford. 136

37. Moreton Old Hall, Cheshire. 136

38. Weatherboarded Houses at Great Wakering, Essex. 138

39. Chequers Court, Buckinghamshire. 138

40. The Queen's House, Greenwich: as originally built. 144

41. The Banqueting House, Whitehall, London. 144

42. Groombridge Place, Kent. 151

43. St. Paul's Cathedral, London, in 1942. 151

44. St. Paul's Cathedral, London: (a) Section; (b) Plan. 154

45. Queen's College, Oxford. 162

46. Chiswick House (the 'Palladian Villa'). 162

47. The Athenaeum Club, London (1830), before alteration. 171

48. Leeds Town Hall (1858). 171

49. The University Museum, Oxford (1860).   179
50. 'Grim's Dyke', Harrow Weald (1872).   179
51. Truro Cathedral (1887–1910).   183
52. Liverpool Cathedral (1904–).   183
53. 'The Orchard', Chorleywood (1900): C. F. A. Voysey's own house.   187
54. House in Church Street, Chelsea: by Mendelsohn and Chermayeff.   187
55. London University: The Senate House.   198
56. The John Ward House, Salem, Mass., U.S.A. (*c.* 1684).   203
57. Westover, Virginia, U.S.A. (*c.* 1726).   203
58. Thomas Jefferson's House (1769–1809) at Monticello, Virginia, U.S.A.   209
59. Presbyterian Medical Center, New York, U.S.A.: Part of First Instalment.   209

CHAPTER I

WHAT IS ARCHITECTURE?

It seems strange that there should be any difficulty in defining the word 'architecture', which has been used in English for some four centuries and in its Latin form was familiar 2,000 years ago, when the Roman architect Vitruvius wrote a book about it under the title *De Architectura*—a book which had an immense vogue during the Renaissance (see p. 125) as well as during his own lifetime. He says that architecture 'consists in applying reason (*ratiocinatio*) to building': in other words, it is logical or intelligent building. An English writer of 1581 defined it as 'the scyence of building'; and the modern *Oxford Dictionary* as 'the art or science of constructing edifices for human use', which is all very well if one is quite sure what 'art' and 'science' mean and is prepared to regard them as synonymous, as few artists or scientists do to-day. Let us take the opinion of Professor W. R. Lethaby (1912), a very wise teacher whose penetrating criticisms will be quoted frequently in the following pages: after discarding various tempting definitions, he concludes that 'it is impossible to differentiate architecture from building'. That is no more helpful for our purpose than this ingenuous statement (1882) by an eminent French archaeologist: 'No satisfactory definition has ever been given of the word "architecture"; and yet, when we use it, everyone knows what we mean.'

On the other hand, Ruskin's view, very prevalent sixty

to eighty years ago, that architecture is 'nothing but ornament added to building', is now rejected by all informed critics. In 1859 James Fergusson, in most respects an admirable historian of architecture, wrote that 'It commences when some embellishment is added to the building which was not strictly a structural necessity'; while Sir Gilbert Scott (the Elder) wrote in 1879 that 'Architecture, as distinguished from mere building, is the decoration of construction.'. Nowadays it is generally agreed that architectural excellence does not depend in the least upon size, cost, or profusion of ornament: all very vulgar criteria.

A much more acceptable and thoughtful view is voiced by Sir Thomas Jackson (1925): 'Architecture is based upon building but is something more than building', as poetry is 'something more than prose'. . . . 'What is it that is added to make the difference?' Then he answers his own question by saying that architecture consists in 'building beautifully, irrespective of all ornament' . . . 'in a word, architecture is the poetry of construction'. A final definition may be quoted from a Polish book published in 1945: 'A technical function carried out by a poet.' Other attempts to define architecture include 'ordered building' (an attractive effort), 'romantic building' (which certainly does not describe all architecture), and—of course—'good building' and 'beautiful building'. The objections to the two last-named are that a building may be weathertight, structurally sound and even functionally efficient without constituting 'good' architecture in the sense that Sir Thomas Jackson has defined it above, while 'beautiful' building throws us right into the prickly field of aesthetics, where every man is apt to consider his judgement as good as his neighbour's and where even professional critics seldom agree, at any rate over any sustained period of time.

We hardly know what men thought of architectural design in the Middle Ages, but when Renaissance ideas were introduced into fashionable circles by the Court in the sixteenth century (p. 126), the medieval tradition that had flourished so happily in England for centuries soon gave way to the new style, and in the seventeenth century our medieval masterpieces—cathedrals and all the rest—were frankly stigmatized as 'barbarous' (p. 85); hence the nickname 'Gothic', first applied as a term of abuse, but eventually coming to denote, for most people in Victorian days, the highest flights of architectural art (p. 181). The pendulum of fashion swung erratically to and fro during the dreary century of 'revivals' preceding the 1914-18 War; and then, between the two World Wars, was nearly jerked off its pin by a startling movement sponsored by political refugees from Germany and elsewhere who, whatever their ability, obviously had no special regard for the English tradition in architecture (p. 195).

In view of all these changes in taste, it might seem impossible to maintain any permanent criteria of 'good' architecture; but, in point of fact, balanced and informed critics of mature judgement are not so easily deflected from their opinions by the ephemeral antics of wild partisans of each fleeting craze, and manage to find something to admire in every one of the slow stages through which architecture has developed during some 3,000 years of history. To me, architecture does mean something more than building: it means building infused with imagination and dignity as well as with technical efficiency; it means, in fact, that it is the work of an artist and an expression of his personality.

*　　　*　　　*

Why, the reader may legitimately ask, does the architect still study the history of his craft while the engineer seldom or never does? Why should this book be so largely concerned with methods of building practised when social needs were so conspicuously different from our own? Those are good questions demanding a considered reply. The answer is that building has evolved very gradually, and that, to understand its modern manifestations, one must know how and why they came about. Engineering, too, has a history, and the modern engineer would benefit, at least as a matter of interest, by devoting more attention to it, thereby humanizing his studies and his work. Moreover, whether we condescend to admire them or not, our country contains a noble series of magnificent buildings of the past, which every Englishman should learn to understand and cherish. Finally, the fluctuations of taste already mentioned become less confusing and perplexing if one really follows the whole story from start to finish.

A brief outline such as this may be written on the basis of form and structure (to which ornament is subsidiary), or on the assumption that architecture is merely a material reflection of prevailing social conditions. Ruskin, taking an 'ethical' line, honestly regarded all Gothic architecture as (morally) 'good', and all Renaissance buildings as unspeakably vile; indeed, he wrote of 'the foul torrent of the Renaissance'. But an impartial study of history does not suggest that favourable social conditions for the people at large invariably produced 'good' architecture. There is no reason why a Conservative Government should not produce buildings as fine as any erected under a Socialist administration; or why either Bolsheviks or Fascists should not create noble architecture. Still less is there any indication that social conditions influenced the actual *form* of architectural features such as vaults and roofs and arches. Naturally the *type* of building erected by an aristocracy (such as that of England or France in the eighteenth century) differed from the type encouraged by the all-powerful Church in the early Middle Ages; and there are other obvious effects, all through history, due to changes in the way of human life. In the limited space available, this little book will give first place to the evolution of architectural form and structure, with appropriate references to the influence of social conditions upon those important aspects.

It is primarily an account of the architecture of the English-speaking peoples, so the story is common for them all up to the settlements of our countrymen in Virginia and New England more than three centuries ago. Thereafter England is treated rather more fully than America, but, as my final chapter makes clear, every oscillation of taste in the Mother Country was matched in the United States. Our own medieval architecture was directly derived from that of Imperial Rome (commemorated by many relics in England), and ultimately from that of Hellenic Greece. Short chapters on Greek and Roman architecture are therefore included; and the next chapter serves as a preface to the work of the Greeks, so that we may penetrate, however hurriedly, to the very root of the genealogical tree.

CHAPTER 2

THE BEGINNINGS

THE FIRST structures erected by man were, of course, rudimentary in form, and do not merit the title of 'architecture'. They were of three main types, according to the materials available locally: (i) mud huts, sometimes with roofs of turf or thatch, developing into brick structures—often roughly domed—as men learned how to mould mud-bricks in the hot alluvial plains of Egypt and Mesopotamia; (ii) stone huts, of the type illustrated in Fig. 1, A, with unhewn stones laid dry in the earliest examples, and often roughly domed; and (iii) structures of timber (Figs. 1, B; 1, C) of various forms. In this latter category are the curious lake-villages of Switzerland and of Glastonbury and Meare in England, built on piles on the shore of a lake or marsh.

It is important to realize that men did not reach the stage of hut-building simultaneously all over the world, or even all over the 'Ancient World'. The nomads of the Middle East still live in tents made of camel-hair, and limestone caves still serve as dwellings in the civilized districts of Normandy and Touraine. The little building illustrated in Fig. 1, B, for instance—'Teapot Hall' in Lincolnshire, which collapsed in 1946—is very primitive, but at most is not older than the fourteenth century. The other example, 1, C, is also late medieval but does approximate to my own minimum standard of 'architecture'. Houses of far more ambitious character than this were raised in the Middle East

6

1. PRIMITIVE BUILDING:

A, Lewis, N.B.; B, Scrivelsby, Lincs.; C, Dymock, Glos.

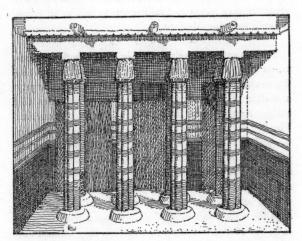

2. PORTICO OF MEHENKWETRE'S HOUSE, c. 2000 B.C.

(From a model in his tomb)

thousands of years ago. On the other hand, Britain possesses some buildings of incredible antiquity, such as the stone huts at Skara Brae in the Orkneys, reliably attributed to *c.* 1500 B.C., and those at Chysauster and Zennor in Cornwall and on Dartmoor, ranging in date from *c.* 1000 B.C. to the first century B.C. The English lake-villages already mentioned probably date from *c.* 100 B.C. For various reasons, the ancient circles and megaliths (='big stones') at Stonehenge and elsewhere in southern England are not described here. They do not appear to me to fall within the main stream of architectural development, although their antiquity and their size are imposing; the same classification applies to such great military works as Maiden Castle and to all forms of prehistoric burial-place.

* * *

The reason why architecture in Egypt and Mesopotamia was so immeasurably ahead of all other parts of the world, 4,000 to 5,000 years ago, seems to be largely a matter of geography. Sir Flinders Petrie dates the earliest relics of man in the Nile valley at *c.* 9000 B.C. The first inhabitants were hunters and nomads, but the marvellous fecundity of the earth (caused by the annual inundation of the river which deposits a thin layer of fresh soil washed down from the remote mountains of Abyssinia) had led them by 9000 B.C. to practise agriculture and to use flint implements. In those far-off days the valley was more thickly wooded than in later ages, but timber was never plentiful; so they utilized the other excellent building materials that lay ready to hand: mud, which they soon learned to mould into bricks and bake in the sun; limestone, which lines both sides of the gorge for most of the 600 miles of its length;

sandstone, which is found in Nubia; and granite, which
occurs at Aswan on the southern frontier of Egypt proper.

The Nile valley is one of the geographical wonders
of the world. Modern railways, and still more recent
motoring roads, have altered conditions to some extent
during the present century; but, even to-day, many
of the primitive methods of agriculture and irrigation
are practised as they were 6,000 years ago. The gorge
averages only twelve miles wide, and on either hand
stretches the barren desert, almost isolating it from
contacts east and west. Everything in life hangs on the
annual inundation—the raising of water by means of
the primitive *shadoof* with its monotonous and melancholy creak, the sowing and gathering of bounteous
crops three times a year. For that reason, among others,
the 'Tyranny of the Nile', as one discriminating critic
has called it, has made itself felt even in Egyptian
architecture, which hardly varied in character, construction, or decoration during an immense span of
years.

Egyptian chronology, by 'dynasties' rather than by
centuries, has always proved a stumbling-block for the
general reader, and all the learned archaeologists who
have written about Egyptian antiquities differ in their
calculations of the earlier stages. The following brief
statement is the result of careful comparison of the
principal rival theories. Of the thirty dynasties from an
uncertain beginning to the Persian conquest of Egypt
in 540 B.C., the first seventeen, prior to *c.* 1550 B.C., are
still very conjectural: from that date onwards, authorities
are in fairly close agreement. The most conservative
estimate of the 1st dynasty is 3400 B.C., the most generous
is 5510 B.C. But these wide deviations need not affect

B

us very much here, if the reader is content to accept my
startling thesis that the pyramids were not architecture
at all, for most of the surviving monuments of the first
seventeen dynasties are pyramids and tombs. There is
a whole chain of pyramids stretching southwards along
the western bank of the Nile for some sixty miles from
the familiar trio at Giza opposite Cairo. Most writers,
Professor Lethaby among them, devote a great deal of
space to this topic, but even he admits that the Great
Pyramid, the largest and most ambitious of all, 'seems
more like a hill of stone than an architectural work'.
More caustic is the opinion of another thoughtful modern
writer: 'A uniform solid triangle of masonry, mechani-
cally accurate and utterly expressionless in its dead
monotony, without any intelligible purpose save the
stupid and ignoble one of hiding a wretched corpse
within its bowels.' With that view I entirely agree, after
some study of Egyptian architecture at first hand. The
pyramids do not come within my own mental definition
of architecture; incidentally they seem to me socially
unjustifiable, in the colossal waste of human life involved
in their erection, and functionally unsound in the
prodigal squandering of means to fulfil their purpose.
As exercises in mysterious geometrical theory, they may
perhaps be deemed interesting.

If, then, we may exclude pyramids and rock-tombs
from the work of the first seventeen dynasties, the only
remaining important monument from that period of
2,000 to 4,000 years is the 'Granite Temple' near the
Sphinx at Giza, an example of enormously solid primitive building. Of the great temples usually visited by
tourists, the fine cluster at Thebes (Karnak, Luxor, Deir
el-Bahari, the Ramesseum, and Medinet Habu) and

that at Abydos date from the 18th-20th dynasties (say 1550-1100 B.C.); while all the remainder (especially at Dendera, Edfu, Esna, Kom Ombo, and Philae) were carried out by the Ptolemaic kings who functioned as Greek satraps from Alexander's conquest of Egypt in 332 B.C. to the Roman conquest three hundred years later. The amazing fact is that Egyptian architecture shows hardly any change from *c.* 3000 B.C. to the Christian era, and the temple at Dendera, erected just before the birth of Christ, might have been built thirty centuries earlier. This is partly what writers mean when they speak of the 'Tyranny of the Nile' in architecture. It impressed Greek travellers of 2,500 years ago just as it impresses us to-day. Nothing changed: it seemed as though nothing could change.

This tyranny was perhaps strengthened by the powerful combination of mythical gods with kings and priests in the religious hierarchy which built the temples and maintained the temple-schools of architecture and building. A people that could worship baboons, crocodiles, vultures, and hippopotami must surely have been lacking in aesthetic discrimination; and in fact the priesthood completely controlled artistic taste. But the changelessness of Egypt is also apparent in the design and decoration of dwelling-houses. Not many of these have survived, for, just as the incredible solidity of tombs, temples, and pyramids shows the importance attached to death and the future life, so the construction of cottages, houses, villas, and even palaces was flimsy in comparison, and they were regarded as temporary 'inns' for the brief life here upon earth. Thus they are known to us chiefly in the beautiful representations of them painted on the walls of the rock-tombs, and in models of houses which were buried in the tombs as part of the miscellaneous assortment of familiar objects to solace the soul of the departed. Fig. 2 shows one such model, of the house of an official in the royal household, about 2000 B.C. There is a forecourt with small flowering trees (not shown on my drawing) and, at the end of it, the verandah or loggia of the house, with rows of columns decorated with 'papyriform' heads. These capitals are sometimes imitated from palm-leaves, sometimes from papyrus flowers, sometimes from lotus flowers: the flowers and leaves may be either open or more usually (as in this case) closed, or in the form of a bud. The shafts of the columns are clustered, and are supposed to be copied from wooden prototypes made of papyrus. All these features go back to the early dynasties, thousands of years before they were used under Greek kings earlier than the time of Christ. Country villas of this type generally contained ten to twenty rooms, grouped round small courtyards, were lavishly decorated, and were surrounded by spacious gardens. A model village of artisan dwellings at Kahun, built for workmen engaged upon a neighbouring pyramid about 4,500 years ago, was laid out on a gridiron plan like an American prairie city; most of the houses contained three rooms and a small yard.

Fig. 3 shows a typical Egyptian temple, viz. the so-called 'Temple of Khons' at Karnak, in the 'hundred-gated city' of Thebes, the capital of Egypt during its chief period of architectural activity, near Luxor on the Nile some 400 miles south of modern Cairo. It shows the essential features of such buildings: the inner sanctuary with its ancillary rooms, the great hall, the pillared courtyard, and the pylon or stone frontispiece of

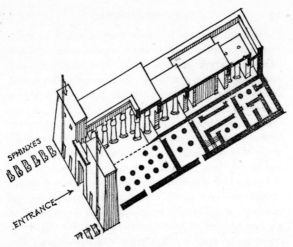

3. SOUTH TEMPLE AT THEBES: SECTIONAL VIEW
(After Choisy)

4. FAÇADE OF THE SHRINE OF ANUBIS AT
DEIR EL-BAHARI

the temple, grooved for huge wooden masts carrying coloured banners. The heavy sausage-shaped columns have papyriform capitals, the roofs are constructed of vast slabs of stone resting on massive stone beams, and avenues of sphinxes lead up to the pylon. The date is *c.* 1200 B.C.

Fig. 4 represents a small part of the huge temple at Deir el-Bahari, also in Thebes, but on the opposite side of the Nile from Karnak. This colossal building, erected during the reign of Queen Hatshepsut about 1550 B.C., covers an area about 200 by 120 yards, and is formally planned on axial lines, with many colonnades like the one illustrated here. It is placed on the lower slope of a rocky hill overlooking Thebes, and stands out dazzlingly white against a background of light brown and orange limestone. The pillars are remarkably like Greek Doric columns of a thousand years later (see Fig. 5), and may well have inspired Greek tourists in Egypt to adopt the same form in their own temples; on the other hand, the Doric Order may have been evolved independently in Hellas. Even this feature can be traced back far beyond the time of Queen Hatshepsut to the beginnings of Egyptian dynastic history.

Add to this the facts that the use of true arches in brickwork is known to be as old as the 3rd dynasty (say 3000-4000 B.C.), that brick barrel-vaults and domes were used about 1500 B.C., and that the shape of a Gothic arch, though not its function, was anticipated at Deir el-Bahari, and it becomes clear that modern European architecture had its beginnings in Egypt. Lack of space forbids any mention here of the methods by which these large, solid, and often elaborate structures were brought into being : the latest works of Sir Flinders Petrie provide a mine of information upon this most enthralling topic, as also upon all the questions of decorative symbolism that can find no room in these pages.

*   *   *

Abreast of this building in Egypt, a parallel advance in architecture was taking place in Mesopotamia, on the shores of the Aegean, and on the island of Crete. Conditions in Mesopotamia resembled those in Egypt, for the fertile plain lying between the rivers Tigris and Euphrates ('Mesopotamia' in Greek means 'between the rivers') was irrigated by them, but was not plentifully supplied with stone as the Nile valley was. Hence mud-brick was the normal building material, and most of the great palaces of the Sumerians, Babylonians, and Assyrians are now mere shapeless mounds of rubble. However, recent excavations have revealed much about their character and history. The Sumerians—the earliest inhabitants of whom we have knowledge—were conquered by King Sargon (possibly 'Nimrod' of the Bible) about 2600 B.C.; thereafter Babylon became the chief city of the region. The principal town of the Sumerians was Ur, on the Euphrates, with two harbours connected by a canal. In its centre was the large temple enclosure or precinct. The remains of the oldest royal tombs found are dated by their discoverer at *c.* 3500 B.C., and clear evidence has been obtained in support of the Old Testament story of the Flood. Ur became important again before the end of the third millennium B.C., when there was built the great *ziggurat* or tower in the temple enclosure, all of brick, and 70 feet square on a base measuring 200 by 150 feet. A facing of glazed brick or faience, which afterwards became a characteristic feature of monumental architecture in western Asia, right up to

modern times; and Sir Leonard Woolley has proved that
here, twenty-three centuries B.C., the 'optical refine-
ments' that are the most remarkable feature of the Greek
Parthenon (p. 25) were anticipated. Other brick
surfaces were gaily painted. Similar characteristics mark
the Babylonian and Assyrian buildings which followed.
Brick arches and vaults were certainly used very early
by the Sumerians, possibly as early as in Egypt. Contact
between the two countries was so frequent that each
influenced the civilization of the other; and Sir Flinders
Petrie thinks that the first rulers of dynastic Egypt came
from Elam, a district of modern Persia bordering
Mesopotamia. It may be added that Babylon was the
largest city of the ancient world, covering an area
$5\frac{1}{2}$ by 3 miles.

In Crete, the third nursery of civilization, the story
begins almost as early as in Mesopotamia and Egypt,
about 3400 B.C., and ends about 1200 B.C. Architectural
interest is confined, so far, to the great palace at Knossos,
sometimes spelt Cnossus, which was mainly erected
during the so-called 'Middle Minoan period', approximately 2100-1580 B.C.: that is, just before Thebes in
Egypt produced its wonderful galaxy of temples and
tombs. It is a large building, about 150 yards square, and
consists of a great number of ceremonial and domestic
rooms grouped round a spacious oblong courtyard. The
religious and official apartments occupied one of the
longer sides; the domestic and residential rooms lay
opposite, across the courtyard. The general lay-out is
relatively formal and imposing, with colonnades and
wide stairs. The principal chambers are elaborately
decorated with fresco-paintings, mainly of natural
subjects such as birds and fishes. There is a most

advanced system of drainage, with closet seats, flushing arrangements, and socketed terracotta drain-pipes: far ahead of anything produced in Europe in the Middle Ages.

There were other early centres of civilization on the shores of the Aegean, at Mycenae, Tiryns, and elsewhere, which had some influence on later Greek ('Hellenic') architecture; and there, as at Knossos, the introduction of architectural features from Mesopotamia, still more from Egypt, has been proved. At Mycenae, a high level of architectural achievement was attained. This Mycenean period, slightly earlier at its beginnings than the presumed but vague date of the Homeric poems, lasted from *c.* 2000 B.C. to *c.* 1000 B.C. At the latter date, the first or 'Dorian' Greeks were making their appearance in Hellas; and at this point our hurried survey of their architectural ancestry must close.

CHAPTER 3

THE GREEKS

IT IS often said to-day that histories of architecture are too much concerned with dates and 'periods', but without some dates the story is apt to meander too vaguely. It is true that precise dates are unimportant to the general reader and even to students up to a certain point; but, because building is an evolutionary process, it is necessary to get its main stages of progression ('periods') into proper sequence in one's mind; and for that purpose the story must be hung on to dates, however approximate, at frequent intervals. The last chapter showed that, in the early stages, dating within reasonable limits is almost impossible, but an important general conclusion emerged, viz. that *c.* 1500 B.C., three mature civilizations were flourishing abreast: at Thebes, the capital of Egypt; in Mesopotamia; and in the island of Crete.

It was at about the same time that the first Aryan Greeks (barbarians at that date) began to trek southwards into Hellas and Asia Minor from the Danube basin. The next significant date to remember is *c.* 700 B.C., when the first important 'Doric' temple was built at Olympia, to be followed within a century by others at Corinth in Greece itself and at Selinus in Sicily. The primitive period of Greek architecture may be reckoned from 700 to 500 B.C., and the 'Golden Age' in Athens occurred in the fifth century, after which a decline began, though the fourth century produced a few notable examples. The period between 1500 and 700 B.C. must have included the Homeric Age, of which the actual date still remains problematical; it saw the gradual collapse of the highly civilized communities at Knossos, Mycenae, and Tiryns; and it also witnessed the transformation of the Greek settlers from blond hunters into organized groups with some skill in the simpler arts and crafts, largely based upon ideas gleaned from their Mycenaean predecessors. One remarkable feature differentiates the Greeks from all other peoples who have figured prominently in history: beginning as small city-states, they federated from time to time as emergency required, but they never coalesced into a nation (much less an empire) until their artificial liberation in the nineteenth century A.D. It is true that the state of Attica, including Athens, may have reached a population of about 350,000 at its zenith, but few other Greek communities exceeded 50,000; and the area of some of these city-states was only a few square miles. Nevertheless, they sent out colonists all over the Mediterranean and the Euxine (Black Sea): thus it is that some of the earliest and finest examples of Greek temples are to be found in southern Italy, Sicily, and Asia Minor. Intercourse between the various 'cities' of Greece was difficult, as the country is very mountainous and there were no roads; so transport was almost entirely by sea. It is extraordinary that this rather heterogeneous assortment of tribes or clans, constantly at war among themselves or with neighbouring states to the east, should have succeeded in attaining a standard of thought, civilization, and art that still serves as a model for the western world. Greece can never have possessed great natural resources, but fortunately there was an abundance of fine marble in her mountains to encourage monumental and durable building.

It is in the temples that the characteristics of Greek architecture can be most easily studied: they form a magnificent series. Greek mythology, if not quite so indiscriminate as that of the Egyptians with its worship of cats and crocodiles, was an amazing ramification of tribal and local deities. There was a class of professional priests and priestesses, but nothing like the rigid and overpowering hierarchy of the Egyptians. The religion of the Greek, writes Sir Reginald Blomfield, 'was not the sinister mystery of Egypt, but on the whole a cheerful open-air Pantheism that gloried in the life and beauty of the visible world in which he lived'. The typical Greek temple is one of the simplest types of building imaginable (Fig. 5). It consists of a sanctuary, the 'cella', with a vestibule at each end, and a colonnade surrounding the whole. There were other types, some of them very small and without the enclosing colonnade, but with a columnar portico at one or both ends. 'Temple B' at Selinus (25 by 15 feet) is no larger than a modern sitting-room, and the famous Temple on the Ilissos at Athens is only 47 feet 6 inches by 25 feet. On the other hand, some of the Greek temples are enormous: e.g. the Temple of Apollo at Miletus, 388 feet long; the Olympeion at Athens, 362 feet (both these including a double colonnade all round the cella); the Parthenon at Athens, 235 feet; and the rather smaller and earlier 'Theseion' at Athens, 109 feet.

The oldest temples of all were built of rough brick and timber, with a stone plinth; and the columns were of wood, with a stone base to protect the foot of each column from damp in the ground. The roofs, from very early

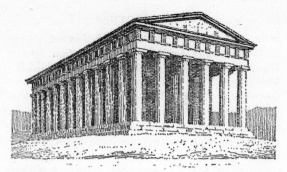

5. THE TEMPLE OF HEPHAISTOS (OR 'THESEION') AT
ATHENS: VIEW AS AT PRESENT

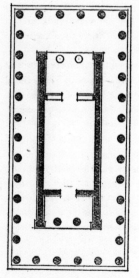

6. TEMPLE OF
HEPHAISTOS: PLAN

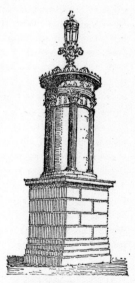

7. MONUMENT OF
LYSIKRATES, ATHENS
(restored)

times, were sloped in two directions, forming a 'span' roof. This feature may have been brought from northern Europe: it differs from the flat roofs used at Thebes, in Mesopotamia, and in Crete. Greek sloping roofs were covered with tiles. Probably the colonnade surrounding the cella originated as 'a sort of verandah to protect its walls' (Lethaby), or as an additional support for the outward-thrusting rafters of the roof. Sometimes there was an additional row of columns or props down the centre of the cella. At each end of the temple was a blank triangular space or gable, terminating the span roof. This came to be known as the 'pediment', and came to be richly decorated with sculpture, free-standing or in high relief. With these few primitive elements, so different from anything preceding them, we have the germ of the Parthenon itself.

As the centuries passed, the whole structure, except the timber roof, was translated into masonry: sometimes only of travertine or other coarse stone, sometimes of stone with a veneer of marble, but, in Athens itself, generally of the lovely honey-coloured marble of Pentelikos. The roof tiles were of Parian marble, but all the roof timbers have vanished, leaving the method of lighting the interior of the cella an unsolved problem. There may have been thin transparent tiles, or some form of clerestory or skylight; but in so brilliant a climate as that of Greece it is conceivable that the sole light within the cella came from the entrance door facing the statue of the god or goddess. Listen to Lethaby on the interior of the Parthenon:

In the interior of the cella there were two rows of columns supporting the roof, and in the farther half of the central space a colossal figure of Athene herself. This amazing statue, the masterwork of Phidias, was formed of casings of gold and ivory over a wooden core; sparkling precious stones were set as eyes into the ivory face, and tresses of wrought gold fell on the shoulders from under a superb helmet. The goddess stood with her left hand on the edge of her round shield, carrying on her extended hand a winged figure of victory. She was the protector of the city who bestowed victory on the Athenians. No light entered the temple save from the great door opposite the figure, which must have been brightly illuminated by many lamps suspended above it. With its blazing eyes, delicate curls of gold, ivory flesh, shining raiment, and added adornment of jewellery and painted details, it went far beyond what we conceive as sculpture: it must have seemed a 'double' of the goddess herself, really dwelling in her temple. A sight of Athene must have been a tremendous experience.

The most prominent feature of a large Greek temple was the colonnade (Fig. 5), and at this point we now encounter a topic which has engrossed so many people and bored so many others: the redoubtable 'Orders of Classical Architecture'. The so-called 'Doric' columns of the Theseion at Athens are of a type familiar to every reader of this book. They acquired their name from one of the primitive Greek tribes—Dorians—who occupied the Peloponnesos (southern Greece) and sundry Mediterranean colonies, whereas the Ionian tribes moved into Attica and Asia Minor. The 'Theseion' at Athens, more probably the Temple of Hephaistos, is the most perfectly preserved of surviving Greek temples, and was finished c. 465 B.C.; that is, just before the Parthenon was begun. It is therefore an example of Greek 'Doric' architecture of the best period. The first thing that may strike a reader on looking at my sketch (Fig. 5) is that the sturdy fluted columns closely resemble those of the

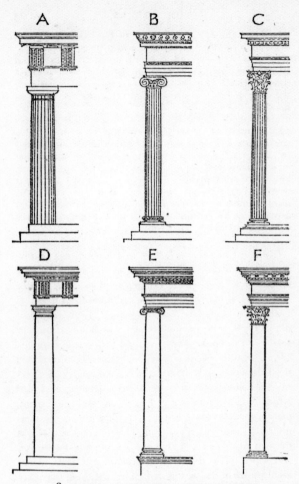

8. ORDERS OF CLASSICAL ARCHITECTURE

THE GREEK ORDERS; A. DORIC; B. IONIC; C. CORINTHIAN

THE ROMAN ORDERS; D. DORIC; E. IONIC; F. CORINTHIAN

Egyptian temple at Deir el-Bahari (Fig. 4), a thousand years older, except that a cushion-shaped capital has been added at the top of the column beneath the square abacus. The 'Doric' columns of the Theseion are $5\frac{1}{2}$ times the height of their lower diameter, and are tapered to give an impression of strength; but this tapering is not a direct diminution from end to end but a diminished swelling known as 'entasis'. This extremely subtle refinement is, however, only one of many devices utilized twenty years later at the Parthenon to correct optical illusions. In archaic Doric columns, the ratio of height to diameter is sometimes much less ($4\frac{1}{3}$ diameters in the Temple of Poseidon at Paestum) or maybe even greater ($6\frac{1}{2}$ diameters at Delphi), and the entasis is less refined than at the Theseion or the Parthenon where the proportions are perfect. At the Theseion the relation of the superstructure of the building (i.e. the heavy stone horizontal beams and cornice supporting the roof, known as the 'entablature') to the lower diameter of the column is exactly 2:1 and at the Parthenon 1·86:1.

Each 'Order' of Greek or Roman architecture (Fig. 8) consists of one type of column—Doric, Ionic, Corinthian—together with its base (if any), its capital, and its entablature. The entablature, in turn, is sub-divided into three portions: the architrave at the bottom, the frieze in the middle, and the cornice on the top. Each of these is subdivided into further sections; and in any manual of the Orders you will find the correct proportions of every part, as determined by long experiment and experience, to produce the ideal visual effect. All the dimensions are given in multiples or fractions of the radius (*not* the diameter) at the base, so that the prescribed rules may be applied to any column in any given building, regardless of its size. Later chapters of this book examine the oft-repeated charge that the Orders, as formulated and taught in later years, came to swamp and stifle all spontaneity and human interest in architecture. At the moment, it is enough to record here that the 'correct' or optimum proportions for Greek Doric, Ionic, and Corinthian columns were the result of centuries of slow experiment and were not formulated or codified at a very early stage. Vitruvius (first century B.C.) tells us, however, that Greek architects hundreds of years before his time did write books about the theory of their craft as well as about their own buildings: unfortunately, all these ancient treatises have been lost, and we have no idea of their scope. It is quite certain that there was nothing hapazard or slapdash about architectural design at Athens twenty-four centuries ago: it was as much a 'science' as an 'art'. Yet nearly all this attention was concentrated upon visual effect. 'It seems clear', says Sir Reginald Blomfield, 'that they devoted most of their attention to the external elevations.' The Greeks did not, like the Romans who followed them, achieve any striking innovations in construction. Indeed they translated into masonry, quite illogically, older timber forms; and Vitruvius explains it all to us, very deliberately, from his standpoint of 2,000 years ago. Where they excelled was in technical perfection of finish, an ideal which their wonderful marble facilitated.

Returning to the Doric column (Fig. 8, A), we see that it stands direct upon the platform (stylobate) of the temple, not upon a small base of its own. The sides of the column are channelled into twenty concave flutings which taper upwards with the delicate entasis of the column. The capital is a plain circular cushion-shaped member, with a very bold projection of parabolic section. (All these Greek sections are very subtle, far more so than in their Roman forms.) The architrave or horizontal beam, above the flat abacus of the column, is absolutely plain. Then comes the frieze, broken up into squares by oblong vertical features—'triglyphs'—representing the ends of timber beams supposed to be resting on the architrave. The square panels—'metopes'—between them are often decorated with sculptured figures in low relief. Lastly comes the boldly projecting cornice, purporting to represent the eaves of a gently sloping roof, with every alternate one of its rafter-feet spaced above a triglyph. Vitruvius explains all this, and there is no reason to suppose that he was romancing. In spite of the imitation of obsolete forms, the total effect of the Doric Order in the best of the temples and elsewhere is most impressive. Besides the 'Theseion' (c. 465) and the Parthenon (454–438 B.C.) at Athens, and the Temple of Zeus at Olympia (472–469), all in Hellas and all of the best period, there are archaic examples at Olympia and Corinth in Greece proper; at Paestum in southern Italy; and at Selinus, Agrigentum, Segesta, and Syracuse in Sicily. In London, the portico of Euston Station is a modern imitation of the Doric Order (cf. p. 173).

The Greek Ionic Order (Fig. 8, B) is far lighter and more graceful than the Doric, with a column eight or nine times as high as the lower diameter. It rests upon a richly moulded base, and the sides of the shaft are divided into twenty-four flutings separated by narrow strips ('fillets'). The striking capital, according to Lethaby, 'is an adaptation of Eastern palm and Egyptian lily capitals'. The spirals or volutes which decorate its corners are a remarkable feature, much simplified when adopted by the Romans in later years, and the palmette ornament between them also comes from the East. The architrave is divided into three recessed stages, capped by a moulding; and the frieze, which has no metopes or triglyphs, sometimes bears a continuous band of sculpture such as may be seen on the Athenaeum Club in London (Fig. 47). The cornice is often elaborately carved and moulded. The Ionic Order originated in the Greek Ionian settlements in Asia Minor, notably in the celebrated Temple of Diana at Ephesus (450 B.C.). A later temple in the same style was erected on the same site; there are other examples at Miletus and Priene in Asia Minor; and in Athens there were the small temples of Niké Apteros (= 'Wingless Victory', 438 B.C.) and on the Ilissos (484 B.C.), as well as the famous Erechtheion (420–393 B.C.), still one of the sights of the Acropolis, but a building of deplorable grouping, notable only for the extreme beauty of its parts. The design of the somewhat depressing church of St. Pancras in London (p. 173) embodies several elements copied from this little temple in Greece.

The third of the trio, the Corinthian Order (Figs. 7 and 8, C), never attained among the Greeks the tremendous vogue it enjoyed under the Romans: indeed it is only found in a few late examples, of which that illustrated is the most important. The chief change occurs in the form of the capital, which is clothed with tiers of spreading acanthus leaves which spring from modified Ionic volutes. A charming but probably quite apocryphal story is told by Vitruvius of the origin of this form, in Corinth; at any rate, it has since been disseminated all over the world. The shaft of the Corinthian column is still more slender than that of the Ionic, being usually about ten diameters in height.

A 'choragic monument' (Fig. 7) was intended to support a bronze tripod, as a prize for athletic or musical competitions in Greek festivals, and an inscription on this example records that 'Lysikrates . . . was *choragos* when the boy-chorus of the phyle Akamantis won the prize', in 335 B.C. It is a graceful little structure, the cylindrical portion being of Pentelic marble and about 9 feet in diameter, on a stone base. The convex roof is a single block of marble, with a wonderful spreading flower of acanthus rising from its centre to carry the tripod, supported by carved brackets of acanthus scrolls.

Of the Greeks' temple architecture, at least, Lethaby is fully justified in writing that they 'first freed the spirit of beauty from the hieratic; architecture was purged of terror; they aimed at what was human, gracious and lovely'. The Monument of Lysikrates gives some idea of their skill in other branches of civic architecture, and Athens in its prime must have been a splendid city so far as civic monuments were concerned. Among other types of public building which can only be mentioned here, but which were found in other cities besides Athens, were the open-air theatre, the odeion or music hall, the stoa or public shelter, the stadion for the athletic contests in which the Greeks revelled, and the hippo-drome for horse-racing. There was a certain amount of formality in the setting of the principal Greek buildings, e.g. a temple was usually surrounded by a temenos or precinct or sacred enclosure; and the great group of monuments crowning the Acropolis (= citadel) of Athens was approached by the magnificent Propylaea in the Doric and Ionic styles. But civic planning as perfected in the later Roman empire was not understood or achieved by the Greeks of the Periclean age in the fifth century B.C.: Greek town-planning, as we define it to-day, is only to be found in the later works of the 'Hellenistic' period, i.e. after the time of Alexander the Great, who founded Alexandria in Egypt in 331 B.C. This was a truly noble city, stretching for miles along the Mediterranean shore, with a population which at one time reached 100,000. The main street, the 'Canopic Way', was four miles long, colonnaded and so well lit at night—by the standards of those days—that an effusive contemporary scribe wrote that it was like 'the sun in small change'. Alexandria was in no way decadent in its prime, and its Museum and Library were world-famous. But now everything Greek above ground has disappeared beneath the buildings of a great modern commercial port. Priene was another well-planned town, and the accidental 'preservation' of Pompeii in southern Italy by a lava-stream has enabled excavators to reveal a great deal about Hellenistic domestic life in 79 A.D., two centuries after Greece itself had become a Roman province.

We are too apt to think of Periclean Athens as a city entirely and superbly built of Parian and Pentelic marble, where incredibly good-looking citizens spouted Socratic dialogue in surroundings of spotless cleanliness and extreme refinement, where man reached his highest level of culture and freedom. In fact, the beautification of Athens by Pericles was largely a measure to relieve post-war unemployment, and upon it he expended all the 'reparations' extorted from the Persians by Athens and her allies. Yet things in his day were probably not quite so squalid as H. G. Wells has pictured them:

Dreaming souls, weary of the vulgarities of our time, have desired to be transferred to the sublime Age of Pericles. But, plumped down into that Athens, they would have found themselves in very much the atmosphere of the lower sort of contemporary music-hall; very much in the vein of our popular newspapers; the same hot blast of braying libel, foul imputation, greedy 'patriotism', and general baseness would have blown upon them, the modern note would have pursued them.

Much in the same style is Bernard Shaw's considered criticism of Periclean buildings as 'umbrella-stand architecture'. But it does seem to be an undeniable fact that the dwelling-houses of most of the citizens were small, dark, cramped, lacking water-supply and drainage and any comforts; and that they stood in narrow, winding, dirty, ill-paved lanes. When the Peiraeus came to be laid out on regular lines at a later date, the Athenians envied its spacious gridiron plan.

Greek architecture, taken as a whole, is a marvel of intellect and skill. Although its designers were certainly aware of the arch and the dome, they ignored them, and were content to develop their 'trabeated' (Latin *trabs* = a beam; hence, post and beam construction) form of building to a point of extreme elegance and logical perfection. It remained for the Romans, as we shall see in the next chapter, to follow up the possibilities of arch, vault, and dome; and to apply to their immense and elaborate monuments much that they had learned from the Greeks.

CHAPTER 4

THE ROMANS

ON MY shelves are two standard histories of Rome. Both end their story with the death of Augustus in A.D. 14; yet that is almost exactly the point when the history of Roman architecture, as represented by existing monuments, begins for us, and indeed it is a commonplace that Augustus is said to have found Rome a city of brick and left it a city of marble. The date when Rome was founded, 753 B.C., seems to be accepted by modern scholars, but the familiar stories of Romulus and Remus, of Horatius 'who kept the bridge in the brave days of old', and so on, are merely amusing and negligible legends. Most of them recall a period when Roman building was limited to primitive huts erected by a small tribe under its chieftain, and even the more ambitious structures of the Republic, after the kings had been expelled in 509 B.C., have mostly disappeared. For all practical purposes, Roman architecture is confined to the buildings of Imperial Rome, and the first 700 years after the city's traditional foundation seem unimportant.

Yet, in that long span of time, Roman architecture had developed and attained maturity, so we must look back beyond the five centuries of the Republic—the glorious years in Roman military history—to the dim shadowy period of the so-called 'Kings', and even further. The first inhabitants of Latium, the district round Rome whence the name 'Latin' is derived, were Italic tribes belonging to the Mediterranean stock. Perhaps about

1000 B.C., invaders began to arrive from northern Europe, attracted by the sunshine of Italy, and settled in the basin of the Po, spreading southwards over the hilly country between the Po and the Tiber, now known as Tuscany. These were the Etruscans, and they probably came to Italy from Asia Minor. Macaulay's *Lays of Ancient Rome* recount the exploits of the primitive Latins in defending their little territory against them. It was a very small kingdom, no larger than one of the lesser English counties, and Rome itself was an insignificant village scattered over the famous 'Seven Hills' at a strategic point commanding a ford across the Tiber, the only considerable river of central Italy. The Etruscans seem to have derived what knowledge of architecture and decoration they possessed from the Greeks, who had established colonies all round the northern shores of the Mediterranean, as we have seen, and they were probably more advanced in their knowledge of building than the Latins can have been at this stage. The earliest known of their monuments are circular tombs (seventh century B.C.), consisting of a stone inner chamber beneath a mound of earth enclosed within a low retaining wall; but, though interesting, these simple structures have little bearing upon our story. Possibly the 'Cloaca Maxima', the large and celebrated stone-arched sewer which drained the marshy ground on which the Romans established their Forum or market-place, dates from the sixth century B.C.; it shows some mastery of arched construction.

When the Roman Republic was founded in 509 B.C., the little town was still primitive, but showed some advance from early days. Its modest houses were of sun-dried bricks with projecting roofs to shield the walls from driving rain, and had small rooms with windows facing inwards on to an enclosed courtyard, the *impluvium*. The roofs were covered with thatch or shingles. The streets were narrow, crooked, and probably very dirty. Between this date and the time of Julius Caesar's assassination in 44 B.C. there was steady progress, but even in 338 B.C. the Roman territory did not extend very far: about a hundred miles along the Mediterranean shore north of Naples, and on an average about twenty miles inland. Sixty years later, Rome controlled all the mainland of Italy south of the Po, and in the first century A.D. the Empire reached its zenith, extending from Morocco to Mesopotamia.

The most rapid development during these six centuries occurred during the second century B.C., when Rome attained the control of the Western world; but the great building boom came rather later, about the time of Christ, when the vast loot of a long series of successful wars was being lavishly expended upon the embellishment of Rome. From the period before Augustus, comparatively little has survived, for all the temples and other buildings erected during the middle and later years of the Republic were replaced by more ambitious structures under spendthrift emperors. The 'Arch of Augustus', one of the city gates of Perugia, is considered to be an early work of the fourth or third century B.C.; and in the garden of the Villa Giulia at Rome is a restoration or reconstruction of an Etruscan temple from Alatri which enables us to-day to imagine what such buildings looked like long ago. It is a simple little edifice with a pair of plain tapered columns at each end, an enclosed cella in the middle, and terracotta ornament of undeniably Greek type on the pediments and along the eaves. There were larger and more imposing temples of this type, in Rome and elsewhere, notably that of Jupiter on the Capitoline Hill, but all have either been rebuilt or have completely perished.

Of the chief surviving monuments of Rome and its colonial cities, including many which are now largely ruined, only a few date from the Republican period in its last phase: all the rest are the work of the long line of emperors, beginning with Augustus in 31 B.C. and ending with Constantine, who transferred the imperial power from Rome to Byzantium in A.D. 330. It is true that Sulla carried out important works in Rome itself, also the wonderful sanctuary of Praeneste on a hill not far away, recently excavated; and that, after him, Julius Caesar remodelled the Forum and erected the great Basilica Julia. But the building boom really began with Augustus, who laid out another Forum, erected several large temples, and—among other things—set up an obelisk from Heliopolis in Egypt, now to be seen in the Piazza del Popolo. His own mausoleum has been recently discovered, and the theatre built in memory of his nephew Marcellus is familiar to most students.

His activities in beautifying Rome were surpassed by some of his successors. His son Tiberius started the fashion for luxurious imperial palaces on the Palatine Hill, and Augustus had occupied a less sumptuous dwelling there himself. In the palaces built subsequently by Nero, Caligula and Domitian, lavish decoration and costly construction was carried to a limit of splendour which can hardly be imagined. Other notable builders among the emperors were Titus, Trajan, and Hadrian; then, after a considerable gap, Diocletian and Constantine.

During this period of nearly four centuries, there were substantial developments in Roman architecture; but its bulk was so enormous and its monuments were of such diverse functional character that it is convenient here to study it first as a way of building, and then to examine in detail the various types of building to which it was applied. Roman architecture is often compared with Greek, generally to the detriment of the former. It is commonly said that the Romans invented the arch, and then applied to honest arched structures the trabeated forms (columns and beams) which they had borrowed from the Greeks, but used them solely for decorative purposes. The Romans are pictured as extremely hard-headed and efficient civil military engineers, the Greeks as highly sensitive artists. In these over-simplified statements there is a measure of truth, but not the whole truth.

In fact, no direct antithesis exists between Roman arched construction and Greek trabeated construction. Lethaby thus defines the position:

Roman architecture is best understood as a form of Hellenistic art imposed on a background which was mostly of Greek origin. Observers of a generation ago [Lethaby was writing in 1911], marking the conflict in mature Roman architecture between arched construction and a superficial application of columns and entablatures, supposed that the arch was indigenous, and that the Orders, taken over from the Greeks, were violently imposed on a native style. Exactly the opposite of this is true. The Greek ideals had long been traditional when arch, vault and dome were brought in by the Hellenistic tide. At the time of Roman expansion the current architecture, having great demands made on it, could not throw off the old wrappings quickly enough; they were, in fact, burst by the new engineering spirit, but vestiges of the old features remained as superficial adornments. This newer and truer view goes very far to relieve Roman architecture of the unfavourable criticism which has been passed upon it. It was not, that is, primarily a system of arched construction which, at a later time, smothered itself under borrowed bedizenments; but it was a phase of Hellenistic art, the result of a transition from the more primitive to the later type of building.

In Chapter 3, it was explained that Hellenistic art was the last phase of the Greek, after Alexander's time; when, as Lethaby puts it, 'a long lingering evening closed in over the Greek world'. Rome *developed* the arch, discovered long before, primarily or partly to serve her new utilitarian needs, but accepted the Greek tradition for such types of building (e.g. temples and theatres) as had already been evolved. Roman civilization differed in so many respects from Greek that modifications of planning and design were involved and many new problems had to be solved. The Etruscans have now come to be regarded, not as originators of a new style, but as the link between Greeks and Romans.

The Pont du Gard at Nîmes in Provence is illustrated here (Fig. 9) as an example of plain arched building on a monumental scale. It was erected in 19 B.C., and carries an aqueduct over a deep valley. There is another fine specimen at Segovia in Spain. Contrasting this illustration with Fig. 10, representing the temple known as the 'Maison Carrée' at Nîmes (A.D. 14), the best-preserved Roman temple extant, we see that the trabeated style used, with the Corinthian Order, differs from Greek examples mainly in the use of a podium (high platform) as a base, instead of spreading steps; and in the fact that the columns at the sides of the temple are half built-in ('engaged') instead of standing free as a 'peristyle' as at the Theseion (Fig. 5); but even that feature had been anticipated by the Greeks in the Monument of Lysikrates (Fig. 7). My point is that the aqueduct was a relatively new type of engineering or utilitarian building; the temple was not.

The chief advance made by the Romans was in the construction of vaults and domes, enabling them to cover great spaces without intermediate supports. Thus the central vault over the Basilica of Constantine at Rome (A.D. 312) is 82 feet wide and is 114 feet high; while the dome of the Pantheon (A.D. 120, Fig 11) is 140 feet in diameter and 140 feet high, supported on walls 20 feet thick. Fig. 12 shows the vaulting over one apartment of the Baths of Diocletian at Rome (A.D. 302) 80 feet wide and 90 feet high, still standing. Nothing like these enormous dimensions had been achieved with trabeated construction. They were made possible by the use of concrete, composed of local lime, volcanic travertine stone for the core, and pozzolana or volcanic ash. The walls of large vaulted structures were also made of concrete, so that the entire building—walls and roof— became a homogeneous whole, without any weak joints. At the same time, there arose a tendency to concentrate the downward thrust of vaults and domes on to piers and columns, and to counteract the outward thrust by means of buttresses, simultaneously reducing intermediate wall areas by recesses and niches. Thus we find the germ of our Gothic system, carried to its highest point in Fig. 29.

Up to the time of Augustus, the emperor who found Rome a city of brick and left it a city of marble, most walls—whether of sun-dried brick or of masonry—had

9. THE ROMAN AQUEDUCT ('PONT DU GARD')
NEAR NÎMES

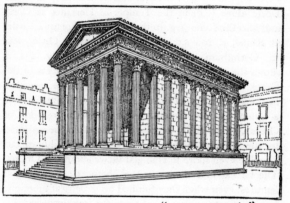

10. THE ROMAN TEMPLE ('MAISON CARRÉE')
AT NÎMES

been coated with thick stucco externally and internally. Vitruvius has much to say about stucco and its composition. From the time of Augustus onwards, stucco was replaced by marble for important buildings; and kiln-dried brick, introduced unaccountably late, was largely used for facing houses and utilitarian structures.

Wooden roof-trusses were often employed, sometimes of very wide span, and roofs were usually tiled, including those over vaults. Domes might also be tiled, or be covered with copper or lead, but it is important to realize that Roman domes were never intended to constitute a feature externally: it was left for Byzantine architects (p. 53), and still more for those of the Renaissance, to develop the dome to the external importance it assumed in our St. Paul's Cathedral and in many other examples elsewhere.

As for the Orders, the Romans occasionally used the Doric alone (e.g. in the Temple of Hercules at Cori) and also the Ionic (e.g. in the Temple of Fortuna Virilis at Rome, *c.* 100 B.C.), but their favourite Order was the Corinthian, which they employed lavishly. Fig. 8 shows the modifications made by their architects to the Greek forms, but a far more drastic change consisted in their use of several Orders in tiers, a practice never adopted by the Greeks. This 'superimposition' of Orders, so generally employed, was often necessitated by the immense height of many Roman buildings but was due even more to changed views about the Orders. The Greeks had always treated them as constructional features, even when they fulfilled no structural function; but the Romans often used them for frankly decorative purposes, to break up large plain wall-surfaces of concrete or stucco. Thus at the Colosseum (A.D 70–82.), the

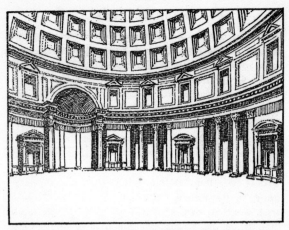

11. THE PANTHEON ROME: INTERIOR

12. BATHS OF DIOCLETIAN, ROME: CENTRAL HALL
(NOW CHURCH OF S. MARIA DEGLI ANGELI)

enormous outer wall of the amphitheatre is 157 feet high, and is decorated with four tiers of Orders, with an arch between each pair of columns. In such cases, the Doric Order is used in the lowest tier as being the sturdiest, then the Ionic, then the Corinthian, and finally—if a fourth Order is needed—the rather flamboyant and feeble type invented by the Romans and known as the 'Composite'. More than 1,500 years later, when the fashion for reviving Roman architecture virulently attacked England, the famous 'Tower of the Five Orders' was built at the Bodleian Library at Oxford (p. 137), the fifth Order being the so-called 'Tuscan' type. Superimposed Orders were used in many buildings, while the traditional fashion of a single Order may be seen in Figs. 10 and 12.

Temples were built in great numbers in Rome itself, and in the fourth century A.D., when the population of the city is computed to have reached a million, Lanciani reckons that Rome contained 400 temples of various types. The simplest rectangular type resembled the 'Maison Carrée' at Nîmes (Fig. 10), but many of the larger examples had a peristyle of free-standing columns all round the central cella or enclosed space, e.g. at the Temples of Mars Ultor, Venus and Rome, etc.; the Great Temple at Baalbek in Syria (A.D. 131–161) had a double peristyle. Some of the largest temples in the whole empire were at Baalbek and Palmyra. In the museum at Colchester in England is a fine model of a large Corinthian temple with a peristyle, built there about A.D. 50 and destroyed by Boadicea a few years later. In more recent times, the Birmingham Town Hall (1832–50) was copied to some extent from the Temple of Jupiter at Rome and has a Corinthian peristyle.

The Romans also favoured circular temples, and these had an important bearing upon later architecture, serving as models for Christian baptisteries. The well-known Temple of Vesta at Tivoli near Rome dates from the time of Augustus, and its design was adopted by Sir John Soane as part of the Bank of England (p. 166). The charming little circular Temple of Vesta in the Forum Boarium at Rome is of the same date. Both these are of the Corinthian Order and each has a peristyle. The Pantheon at Rome (Fig. 11) is one of the great architectural masterpieces of the world and was built in A.D. 120–124. Its construction has already been mentioned, and the illustration gives some idea of the interior, but does not show the large circular unglazed opening in the top of the dome which affords the only light. It is 27 feet in diameter. The bold 'coffering' of the internal surface of the dome should be noted. Externally the building is plain and has no peristyle, but there is a fine Corinthian portico. There is another circular temple at Baalbek, and Diocletian's Palace at Spalato in Dalmatia contains an octagonal temple.

Roman theatres followed Greek precedent to some extent, but there were some differences in the arrangement of the auditorium. The Theatre of Marcellus (23–13 B.C.) is the only example in Rome, but there is a good specimen at Orange in France (c. A.D. 120) holding some 7,000 spectators; and in England a smaller one at Verulamium (St. Albans), built c. A.D. 140–150, which provided about 1,600 seats. More characteristic of Imperial Rome are the enormous amphitheatres erected for the often bloodthirsty spectacles beloved of the populace during the long period of Rome's luxury and decline. The nature of such spectacles will be familiar to most readers and cannot be described here. The so-called 'Colosseum' in Rome, more correctly the Flavian Amphitheatre (A.D. 70–82), is and was the largest of all, with accommodation reckoned at 45,000 seats plus room for some 5,000 spectators standing. Its exterior has already been described. The amphitheatres at Verona in Italy, Nîmes and Arles in Provence, hold 20,000, 24,000, and 26,000 persons respectively; and the smaller example at Caerleon in Monmouthshire (late first century A.D.) is impressive enough.

Another feature of Rome, and found elsewhere, is to be seen in the fine triumphal arches raised to commemorate the successful conclusion of military campaigns. Some of these consisted of a single arch, e.g. the Arch of Titus in Rome (A.D. 81) and those at Ancona (113) and Benevento (114). Others, e.g. the Arches of Septimius Severus (204) and Constantine (Fig. 13) in Rome and that at Orange in France, had three arches. From the latter type the 'Marble Arch' in London was derived.

Splendid as were these great monuments of stone and marble, they were completely outclassed by the series of huge Thermae built by the more prodigal emperors. Theoretically bathing establishments, they were, in fact, enormous popular clubs where almost any citizen was free to enter and where he could amuse himself all day. Each of them consisted of a range of vast halls, vaulted or domed, and the newly developed system of concrete vaulting enabled the architects to create diversity in their planning by varying the shapes and sizes of rooms, any of which they knew they could roof. The largest of these Thermae were erected by Caracalla (A.D. 212–235) and Diocletian (A.D. 302): the central hall of the latter is illustrated in Fig. 12. It was converted into a church by

13. THE ARCH OF CONSTANTINE, ROME

14. FLATS AND SHOPS AT OSTIA, NEAR ROME
(restored)

Michelangelo in 1563. This single room is 200 feet long and 80 feet wide. The main columns are Egyptian granite monoliths with white marble capitals.

The palaces of the emperors have already been mentioned, and the mansions of the wealthier citizens were sumptuously built, but it seems unlikely that the poorer classes were adequately housed. Pompeii, though a Hellenistic city, sheds a sidelight on Roman home life; and Britain contains a number of spacious 'villas' or country-houses (e.g. at Chedworth, Folkestone, Brading) with mosaic floors, central heating, baths, and other indications of a highly civilized life. In Rome itself, and in its maritime suburb of Ostia, many people lived in flats or apartment-houses, of surprisingly modern appearance (Fig. 14).

In the matter of civic adornment, Rome itself was magnificent, but this aspect of town-planning may be studied more effectively in the great cities of Syria and North Africa, now deserted and ruined, e.g. Baalbek, Palmyra, and Timgad. One important type of building has not been described in this chapter, viz. the basilica or hall of justice, although splendid examples exist in Rome. The reason is that they are chiefly interesting to us to-day, apart from their construction, as prototypes of the early Christian churches to be discussed in the next chapter, and are therefore better mentioned there.

All that we owe to the Romans in architecture [wrote Lethaby] may hardly be recounted. They absorbed all the traditions of antiquity and renewed them into modern shape. Their ideal of construction was the most perfect and generally applicable that may be imagined. A typical Roman building was of one piece, an artificial monolith. . . . In Roman architecture the engineering element is paramount. It was this which broke the moulds of tradition and recast construction into modern form and made it free once more. . . . With all this mechanical perfection it must be confessed that there remains in the architectural expression of Roman works something which is not truly fine. They stand for force, expansion, splendour; the art was official, self-satisfied, oppressive. It gives a voice to matter as Greece had expressed mind. Rome was lacking in the things of the spirit. There is little wonder—the first early wonder at mysteries—left in Roman art; the dew of the morning is dried up; it is the great Philistine style.

CHAPTER 5

THE DARK AGES

THE TITLE of this chapter is doubtless open to criticism, and indeed is seldom used by modern historians, though such eminent Victorians as Hallam, Buckle, and Maitland employed it a century ago. It is introduced here to cover the long and confused period of more than seven centuries between Constantine's transfer of the capital of his empire from Rome to Byzantium in A.D. 330 and the Norman conquest of England in 1066. The title 'Early Christian' does not satisfactorily describe its architecture, for the rise of Islam occurred in the seventh century with its considerable influence on building in Europe, and the phases of architecture known variously as Byzantine, Lombard, Romanesque, and Saxon are all involved; so some short inclusive title, however unacademic, is required. The period was certainly 'dark' in the sense that it witnessed the 'Decline and Fall of the Roman Empire' recorded for all time in Gibbon's noble history, with all the accompanying misery, destruction, ignorance, and obscurantism caused by the barbarian invasions of Europe; on the other hand, it also saw the evolution of early church building and the establishment of the monastic orders.

As previously explained, this book is primarily concerned with English architecture and its origins. The foregoing chapters have therefore dealt with the ultimate sources of our architecture in Rome, Greece, and even in remote Egypt; and no mention has been made of

English buildings except incidental references to Roman remains in the last chapter. It would have been possible to pass directly from Colchester, Silchester, and Verulamium to the first post-Roman architecture—Christian or 'Saxon' churches erected from the seventh century onwards—without regard to the progress of architecture in Continental Europe; but that method, if easy because it avoids any allusion to the complicated world-history of the period, is also unscholarly, for the course of evolution in building design and construction abroad had a direct bearing upon English architecture of the 'Saxon' and subsequent phases. After the present chapter, the story will be confined to England, one single branch of the many-branched architectural tree which had its roots in the fertile mud of the Nile valley 4,000 years ago. But, in this chapter, we must trace the first stages of growth—from the main trunk—of some four separate branches before we can understand the great achievements of Norman architecture in our own land. These separate phases are: (1) the evolution of Christian church building, particularly in Italy, from Constantine's day; (2) similar progress under the later or 'Eastern Roman' emperors whose capital was at Byzantium, rechristened 'Constantinople'; (3) the early mosques erected by the Muslims in countries conquered from the Romans and Byzantines; and finally (4) the early so-called 'Saxon' churches built in England between St. Augustine's landing in A.D. 597 and the Norman Conquest in 1066.

*   *   *

For the first three centuries after the time of Christ, His followers in Rome, as elsewhere, were compelled by intermittent but savage persecution to conduct their worship 'underground', in our modern phraseology, and sometimes quite literally underground. No sensitive and imaginative visitor to the catacombs of Rome can emerge utterly unmoved from those immense subterranean burial-places with their pathetic carved inscriptions. 'You know the days of our meetings', complained Tertullian to his Roman judges at the end of the second century; 'You have your eye upon us even in our most secret meetings, so you often come to surprise and overwhelm us.' Sometimes a whole congregation of men, women, and children was thus taken unawares and immured alive.

As at a much later period when English Dissenters were hunted and persecuted, religious meetings were frequently held in private houses; and, though there are a few literary records of the erection of church buildings in the Roman provinces, these were uncommon before the middle of the third century, when many were built just before the last persecution in 303, but no vestige of them remains except the foundations of a very primitive building adjoining, and partly overlaid by, the cathedral at Parenzo in Istria. It was a simple rectangle, 75 by 26 feet, and A. W. Clapham has aptly compared it to the English meeting-houses erected by the Congregationalists, Presbyterians, and Quakers after the Toleration Act of 1689 permitted Nonconformists to construct buildings for worship (cf. p. 155).

The same author comments upon the fact that, when Constantine embraced Christianity himself in 323 and allowed Christian churches to be built throughout the Empire, the series of great 'basilicas' that were erected almost immediately in Rome displayed a uniformity of design and ritual arrangement that would seem to imply

some earlier process of evolution for which no evidence
survives.

The origin of the church plan [writes Lethaby] has
been endlessly discussed. Some scholars would derive it
from the atrium and reception-hall of the Roman house.
Some would see other elements, taken over from the
temple and the synagogue. The most typical early
church plan consisted of a forecourt, a nave with pillars,
and an apse. This is the 'basilican' plan. A Roman
basilica, or justice-hall, approximated to this form, and
the word 'Basilica' seems to have had a general meaning
like our word 'Hall'. The civil basilica was anciently the
public portico where the chief magistrates administered
justice. It was afterwards enclosed like a temple, and
adapted to various uses. One custom which the church
certainly derived from temple architecture is that of
orientation, or planning the building on an east-to-west
axis.

Clapham states: 'The old theory that pagan and secular
buildings were handed over to the Christians for transformation into churches has long been exploded.'

The great basilican churches erected in Rome were
St. Peter's (330, completely rebuilt in Renaissance
times); S. Giovanni in Laterano (330, much altered
since); S. Paolo fuori le Mura (380, burned down 1823
but then rebuilt precisely in its original form); S.
Clemente (392, rebuilt); S. Maria Maggiore (432,
much altered externally, but retaining its interior
unchanged); S. Lorenzo (432, much altered); S. Sabina
(425, much altered, see Fig. 15); and S. Agnese (625).
Outside Rome the chief examples are S. Apollinare
Nuovo (493–525) and S. Apollinare in Classe (534–49)
at Ravenna, the Cathedral at Parenzo (c. 530, Fig. 16),
the partly rebuilt little Cathedral at Torcello near

Venice (864 and 1008), and the Church of the Holy
Nativity at Bethlehem (begun 327). Lethaby says of
this last 'noble and impressive building' that it is 'the
most perfect existing early Christian church'.

Of the examples in Rome, S. Sabina (Fig. 15) now
possesses the most typical primitive interior, as sundry
later features were removed when restoration took place
in 1919. It has a central nave with side-aisles, separated

15. BASILICAN CHURCH OF S. SABINA, ROME:
INTERIOR

by ranges of Corinthian columns, from which spring
semicircular arches, the first instance of this treatment
found in Roman churches. The columns seem to have
been taken from a neighbouring pagan temple, so
are older than the church itself. Above the arches are
round-headed clerestory windows. The low-pitched roof
is carried on massive timber trusses. At the east end of
the nave is an apse, a feature usually decorated with
mosaics depicting Christ in glory. Low marble walls

enclose a chancel, in which are twin pulpits known as *ambones* (plural of *ambo*), a characteristic feature of these early churches. Most of these early churches were approached through an atrium or forecourt, surrounded by an arcade and forming a cloister (Fig. 16). The part of the atrium adjoining the church was known as the narthex or vestibule.

Another type of Christian church built during this period was circular or polygonal in form. This was derived, according to Lethaby, from Roman tombs. The most perfect example is S. Costanza at Rome (*c.* 354); another example in Rome is S. Stefano Rotondo (470); also the Baptisteries of Constantine at Rome (430) and Nocera (350); and that at Ravenna. A third form, the *cella trichora*, with a simple nave and a cluster of three apses at the end, probably originated in burial chapels.

* * *

Byzantine architecture, as its name implies, was the phase which Roman architecture assumed in the eastern provinces after Constantine transferred the seat of government to Byzantium. Its influence on English architecture was relatively slight and never direct, but Byzantine ornamental *motifs* found their way into England by devious routes in a most extraordinary way during the latter part of the 'Dark Ages', and may be seen on sculptured crosses in our northern counties (p. 62).

The simplest form of the Byzantine mode [writes Lethaby] is to be found in the substitution of the domed and vaulted church for the wood-roofed basilica. This change probably had its origin in Christian Egypt, where domical roofing seems to have been indigenous, and where from time to time it would be applied to new purposes.

16. PARENZO: ATRIUM OF THE CATHEDRAL

He adds that carved capitals from Christian churches in Egypt, probably of the fifth century, may well be the prototypes of 'the noble Constantinopolitan marble capitals' in the glorious church of S. Sophia (537), which he proceeds later to describe.

The great central cupola is surrounded by lower semi-domes and domes of various sizes, which heave up above one another like a cluster of bubbles. The church of S. Sophia is one of the great things of all time. It is very large, yet it is a unit, not an aggregation of many parts. The central area, over 100 feet square, is extended to the east and the west by great hemicycles, which increase the length of the central hall to over 200 feet. From these hemicycles smaller apses break out, and along each side of the central area there are vast aisles supporting galleries. The size is gigantic, the more so as Byzantine churches are small, with this one exception.

Among smaller examples are the churches of SS. Sergius and Bacchus (527) and of S. Irene (740) at Constantinople, of S. Sophia (560) at Salonica, and of S. Vitale (526-47) at Ravenna, a most remarkable building. St. Mark's at Venice (1042-71) is far more famous and far larger than any of these, but has been so smothered by later florid Gothic additions that its external appearance has been entirely altered.

*   *   *

About a century after the time of the emperor Justinian, who built S. Sophia, his Eastern Roman Empire was shaken to its foundations by the sudden rise of Islam, the religious movement founded by Muhammad in Arabia in A.D. 622. At that time, the Byzantine Empire included the whole of the Balkan peninsula, Asia Minor, Arabia, Iraq, Persia, Egypt, and

Syria. Most of the remainder of North Africa was under Vandal rule, and Spain was occupied by the West Goths. In little more than a century the Muslim Arabs had conquered the whole of this vast area, except the Balkan peninsula and part of Asia Minor, over-running all the elaborate system of civilization established by the Romans centuries before. Alexandria, the home of Hellenistic art, was among their earliest captures, and many other rich cities fell into their hands. Essentially warriors imbued with a fanatical faith, they had no skill in architecture or any of the arts, so they utilized the talents of designers and craftsmen from all the conquered provinces. They also looted impartially both pagan temples and Christian churches to obtain materials for their places of worship—mosques—with the result that many of their earliest buildings have colonnades composed of a motley assortment of Roman marble columns, of varying lengths, with additional bases used to produce a uniform height. Even in matters of design, they relied at first upon Christian craftsmen.

The earliest Arab works [writes Lethaby], like the Dome of the Rock (seventh century) and the Mosque of Aksa in Jerusalem, and the Great Mosque at Damascus (*c.* 710) are almost perfect Byzantine buildings, except for touches of added energy.

That is not the whole truth: almost from the beginning, the Arabs made use of the pointed arch in their buildings, certainly at Damascus. As we have seen, it had been employed at a very early period elsewhere, but not on the scale now adopted and not generally in a structural form. Thus it happens that we find whole arcades of large pointed arches in Muslim mosques of the Middle

17. MOSQUE OF IBN TŪLŪN, CAIRO:
ARCADE IN SANCTUARY

East two centuries at least before they appeared in England and Western Europe, to become eventually the characteristic and dominant feature of our Gothic architecture. Fig. 17 illustrates part of the large mosque of Ibn Tūlūn at Cairo, built 876–9 and covering 6½ acres of ground. The sanctuary on one side of the enormous central courtyard has five ranges of arches like the one illustrated, with seventeen arches in each range; and there are double rows of arches round the three remaining sides of the courtyard. Arches and piers are of brick, coated with stucco, and there are (imitation) 'engaged' shafts at the angles of the piers. The roofs are, or were, of horizontal wooden logs covered with earth and are panelled internally. The outer walls of the mosque contain pointed windows filled with delicate stucco tracery in geometrical patterns, and terminate in battlements of a curious saw-tooth form. All these features are derived from Iraq (Mesopotamia), where brick architecture had made great strides under the Sassanid dynasty (A.D. 226–641), and not from Roman sources. The importance to us of this remarkable building, erected in the time of our King Alfred when English architecture was at a rudimentary stage, is that it anticipates by centuries several noteworthy 'Gothic' features. It was not the first of its kind, but there is no need to give a list here of other famous early Islamic buildings, though perhaps the Great Mosque of Cordova in Spain (begun in 786) should be mentioned as an example within the confines of western Europe.

* * *

Having thus travelled so far from England, we may now return home, pausing only to inquire what was happening in France and Germany since the collapse of Roman rule during the fifth century. France was gradually occupied by Frankish tribes, and with it western Germany, Belgium, and Holland. By the time of Charlemagne (768–814), the Frankish kingdom included modern Switzerland, Bavaria, Austria, and Italy as far south as Rome. Yet in this wide area and from so long a period, hardly a building older than the eleventh century survives to-day, almost the only exceptions being Charlemagne's own cathedral at Aachen (796–804) and a small but very interesting church at Germigny des Près (801) in France, showing Islamic influence. Conditions of life in western Europe must have been precarious indeed during this era of chaos, and the epithet of the 'Dark Ages' may be justified, at any rate as applied to architecture.

To some extent, the same thing is true of England; but, nevertheless, every Englishman with a sense of patriotic imagination must be stirred by the earliest monuments of his forebears, meagre as they may be in artistic merit as they certainly are in size. Without exception, they are churches of some sort: monasteries or cathedrals or parish-churches. The rude dwellings of our ancestors, even their castles, have long since disappeared. Shortly before the last of the legions left our shores in A.D. 410, a little Christian church had been built in the Roman town of Silchester near Reading, and its foundations still remain among the relics of what one authority has described as 'something of a garden city', composed of eighty houses disposed, with an acre of land to each, on the usual rectangular street-plan. It was a very small church, to suit so scanty a population, measuring only some 45 feet in length externally, and had a nave terminating in an apse, with side-aisles, transepts, and a narthex. The floor was paved with red *tesserae* (mosaic squares). This tiny building was excavated in 1892.

Then follows a gap of about two centuries, covering the period of the Anglo-Saxon invasions, until the next period of church building, which followed St. Augustine's landing in Kent in 597 and his speedy conversion of the Kentish king. To the seventh century belong a group of seven small churches, all but one in Kent. They are SS. Peter and Paul, St. Mary, and St. Pancras at Canterbury; St. Andrew at Rochester; St. Mary at Lyminge; St. Mary at Reculver (*c.* 670); and St. Peter at Bradwell on the Essex coast (*c.* 660). All have apses, and those of St. Pancras and Bradwell have aisles. Most are mere ruins, but that at Bradwell is intact save for its apse and *porticūs* (transeptal projections).

SS. Peter and Paul at Canterbury, like that of Reculver, had a western narthex, and there is a record that one of the two *porticūs* contained the tombs of St. Augustine and his successors in the See of Canterbury, the other the tombs of the Kentish kings, while each *porticūs* also contained an eastern altar. Thus we have the nucleus of the Gothic church-plan, obviously derived from the Roman basilicas which St. Augustine had seen in Rome, but on a much smaller scale. It seems probable that among the men who accompanied him were refugees driven from Italy by the barbarian invasions, including the architects and builders who directed the erection of these simple structures. The small church at Reculver, foolishly demolished in 1805, had two columns of the Roman Doric Order, now preserved in the precinct of Canterbury Cathedral. Its walls were of Roman brick and rubble, some portions of which still remain. The use of *porticūs* is common in churches of the fifth and sixth centuries in Syria and North Africa. The significance of this little group of churches is stressed by Clapham, who states that: 'It is not too much to say that in no other part of Western Europe do there now survive so many examples of a like age in so small a geographical compass.'

In the latter part of the seventh century, several more churches were built in southern England, including a very large one at Abingdon (*c.* 680), with apses at both ends, now completely destroyed; the small church of St. Martin at Canterbury; and the fine church at Brixworth in Northamptonshire (*c.* 670), described by Clapham as 'perhaps the most imposing architectural memorial of the seventh century yet surviving north of the Alps', and still standing in excellent preservation, though considerably altered and now lacking its aisles. It is of basilican form and has some affinity to the Kentish group just mentioned. Its total length is the same as that at Abingdon, about 120 feet plus a small apsidal chancel, polygonal externally. The nave has four bays of massive brick arches resting on piers, with clerestory windows above and a timber roof. East of this is a square presbytery without aisles. The workmanship of the arches is so unskilled that experts believe it to have been executed by native masons rather than by Italian craftsmen; for the 'Dark Ages' that followed the Roman evacuation of Britain had produced no stone building, and the art of masonry had been lost. This church originally had a western narthex, of which only a portion survives.

The next group of churches was built at the end of the seventh century in 'Northumbria', then, as its name implies, a separate kingdom extending from the Humber to the Firth of Forth. They are considered to be the work of Benedict Biscop, a scholarly Englishman who brought masons from Gaul for the purpose and instructed them to build 'after the manner of the Romans' (*more Romanorum*). As hardly anything remains of early churches in France, we cannot make comparisons between Northumbrian and Gaulish examples, but the former are of more rustic construction and design than the Kentish group. Those remaining consist of the small church of Escomb in the county of Durham, with an aisleless nave and a tiny square-ended chancel; the aisleless nave of the church at Monkwearmouth in the county of Durham, with a two-storied west porch roofed with a barrel-vault, and two *porticūs*; the small church at Corbridge in Northumberland; and possibly the existing chancel (formerly the aisleless nave) of the church at Jarrow. The masonry of all these buildings is rough, and the only remarkable features are the barbaric carvings and the turned stone balusters of the church at Monkwearmouth. The crypts built by St. Wilfrid, archbishop of York, at Hexham and Ripon are all that survive of the large churches erected by this prelate at about the same period.

The fine stone crosses still to be seen in sundry northern churchyards have no direct bearing on the history of architecture, but are of outstanding interest in that they provide evidence of the transmission of artistic *motifs* from eastern Europe to remote parts of Britain. Oddly enough, they supply the decorative factor which is entirely lacking in the well-built Saxon churches of Kent. It seems that St. Augustine brought no sculptors in his train, but Theodore of Tarsus (in Asia Minor) and

Adrian, who came with him to England in 669 as a refugee from the Muslims in North Africa, may have been accompanied by sculptors from the East. At any rate, these early crosses are carved with ornament of Byzantine type; and the oldest example, at Otley in Yorkshire, has vine-scrolls resembling those on the ivory throne of Ravenna, a work ascribed to the fifth or sixth century and possibly made at Alexandria. The finest specimens are at Ruthwell in Dumfriesshire; at Bewcastle in Cumberland; and at Croft, Easby, and Hovingham in Yorkshire. The great Acca's Cross at Durham (formerly at Hexham) and that at Abercorn in Midlothian are rather later in date. There are also several examples of the late eighth and ninth centuries in the North Midlands and Lancashire: notably the crosses at Sandbach (Cheshire); Eyam, Bakewell, and Bradbourne (Derbyshire); Irton (Lancashire); and Stapleford (Nottinghamshire).

After the coronation of Charlemagne in 800, conditions in western Europe became more stable, putting an end to the previous state of chaos; but few if any remains of ninth-century churches exist in England. At Elmham, in mid-Norfolk, are the ruins of a former cathedral, probably built late in the tenth or early in the following century. It had a long nave, a transept, two transeptal towers, a large western tower, and an apse, but no aisles. At Peterborough and Glastonbury, remains of large tenth-century churches have recently been unearthed. Deerhurst in Gloucestershire has a fine church with an aisleless nave, a polygonal apse, and transeptal chapels; also a western tower, still standing. At Wing in Buckinghamshire is a splendid Saxon church with an aisled nave and a polygonal apse or chancel. The charming little church of Worth in Sussex (tenth century) is of great interest for its details as well as its plan. It has an aisleless nave, transepts, and a deep apsidal chancel, all in very good preservation.

Fig. 18 gives a view and plan of the tiny church at Bradford-on-Avon in Wiltshire, a work of the early tenth century. (The plan is reversed to comply with the view, taken from the south-east.) Very unusually, it is built of 'ashlar' (cut stones) instead of rubble. It is very narrow and lofty internally, with a steep roof and without an apse. The exterior is decorated with shallow arcading, a feature much favoured in the Rhineland and Lombardy, the two areas of continental Europe where building was proceeding briskly at this date. For centuries this little building had been used partly as a school and partly as a dwelling with floors inserted in the chancel, its original purpose having been completely forgotten; until in 1856, according to the official guidebook, the then Vicar, 'looking down upon it from the top rank of houses, noted the cruciform roofs and sprang to the conclusion that it must be the church which was known to have stood on that site'. Restoration took place in 1871, and the result appears in my sketch.

The other example illustrated (Fig. 19) is the Saxon tower of the church at Earl's Barton in Northamptonshire, a work of the tenth century, which exhibits several characteristics of the period. (The battlements are a late Gothic addition.) The rubble stone walls are panelled with stone pilaster-strips serving no structural purpose, and with rudimentary arcading. This form of decoration is supposed to be of Roman origin via the Rhineland. The angles of the tower walls have alternate long and short 'quoins' (corner-stones), used decoratively

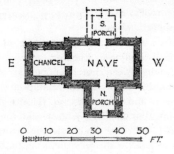

18. CHURCH OF ST. LAWRENCE, BRADFORD-ON-AVON

here but originally of some structural value in rubble walls. Most of the small and narrow windows are divided by turned baluster-shafts and have semi-circular heads, but some have triangular heads. All these features are repeated in the coeval church-tower at Barton-on-Humber, Lincolnshire; but the most interesting tower of all is to be seen at Sompting in Sussex (early eleventh century), where a pyramidal roof rises from high-pitched gables

19. EARL'S BARTON CHURCH, NORTHANTS

on each face: this is a characteristic of Rhenish churches, but is unique in England.

Other surviving Saxon churches of note are at Barnack (Northamptonshire), Breamore (Hampshire), Bishop-stoke (Sussex), and Great Paxton (Huntingdonshire). The crypt at Repton (Derbyshire) and the tower of St. Benet at Cambridge should also be mentioned. At Greenstead in Essex is the only surviving timber church of Saxon date, built of split oak logs, but timber churches were numerous before the Norman Conquest. The foregoing account of Saxon architecture, brief as it is, may be considered unduly lengthy for so small a book, but the interest of these little churches as our oldest architectural monuments must serve as my excuse.

CHAPTER 6

NORMAN ARCHITECTURE

THE TERM 'Norman', which has been used to describe the 'form of architecture developed by the Normans and employed in England after the Conquest' (*Oxford English Dictionary*) since 1772, is now generally discarded by serious historians in favour of the more inclusive word 'Romanesque', applied in general to 'the buildings erected in Romanized Europe between the close of the classical period and the rise of Gothic architecture' (*O.E.D.*): sometimes, but not always, including the Early Christian churches but usually excluding Byzantine architecture. Thus it also embraces the 'Saxon' style discussed in Chapter 5, and in his work on *Romanesque Architecture in England* A. W. Clapham entitles his two volumes *Before the Conquest* and *After the Conquest* respectively, thereby admitting the importance of the Conquest as a landmark. For the purpose of my little book, concerned as it is primarily with England, it is convenient to adopt the older terminology, however obsolete it may be regarded by the learned, and to admit that our Norman architecture had a distinctive character of its own.

We must first consider the Normans, and next what was the state of architecture in Continental Europe, whence they came, in 1066. The word 'Normans', as every schoolboy knows, is a contraction for 'Northmen', and denotes all the wandering Scandinavian pirates and adventurers who harried our English coasts from the closing years of the eighth century onwards. Sometimes they are called 'Vik-ings', the men of the fiords or creeks (*vik* = inlet in Old Norse). As their confidence and their maritime skill increased, they penetrated to many other parts of Europe besides our own shores: to Kiev and Novgorod in Russia, even to Sicily and the remote 'Heel of Italy', where they established various principalities during the eleventh century, so that in those distant places we may still find beautiful 'Norman' churches closely resembling our own. But, of course, their most important settlement before 1066 was in the part of France which they first occupied in 911, known ever since as Normandy. Their capital was at Rouen. In a characteristically sonorous passage, Gibbon describes their gradual conversion to Latin culture:

The savage fierceness which they had brought from the snowy mountains of Norway was refined, without being corrupted, in a warmer climate; the companions of Rollo [Duke of Normandy] insensibly mingled with the natives; they imbibed the manners, language and gallantry of the French nation.

Moreover, 'they renounced their gods for the God of the Christians'. Yet a more recent historian, Professor Trevelyan, has explained that their emergence from barbarism was slow:

They were not what we should recognize as a civilized people In spite of a few learned priests, the upper class were ignorant of the rudiments of letters; there were no lawyers and practically no professional men except the clergy; the luxury, art, commerce, and chivalry of the later Middle Ages had not yet come into existence, and nothing of that kind was to be found in the timber fortresses and occasional stone 'donjons' of this primitive baronage.

The enormous number, the impressive size, and the rich details of the buildings erected by the Normans in England within half a century of the Conquest suggest that the invaders had slowly developed a high degree of architectural skill during their long sojourn in France, before they crossed the Channel into Sussex; but the fact seems to be that this development took place very rapidly, during the few years immediately before the Conquest, and proceeded quite as rapidly in England, once it was transplanted here, as in its original habitat. As stated in Chapter 5, architecture in western Europe during the period before A.D. 1000 has left us very few surviving examples. Many early buildings of importance were demolished during the later Middle Ages in favour of more imposing structures, and this applies particularly to the chief monastic churches, for monasticism was powerful in Europe long before the Norman Conquest. Only in northern Italy and the Rhineland can we still see a few noteworthy buildings that may conceivably have inspired the Normans during the half-century preceding their conquest of England, but the influence of Rome was there nevertheless. Probably the larger Saxon churches in this country, such as that at Brixworth, and the much larger cathedrals and monastic churches since demolished or rebuilt, displayed as high a degree of skill as any Romanesque building in France erected before 1000; so we must attribute the remarkable achievement of the Normans in architecture, immediately before and after the Conquest, to the energy of their native character even more than to Carolingian skill or to Roman tradition.

The Norman form of Romanesque [writes Lethaby] was introduced into England when Edward the Confessor rebuilt Westminster Abbey from about 1050 to 1066. Chroniclers say that no church like it had before been seen. Several years ago I suggested that it was probably copied from the Abbey of Jumièges, and further research has proved this to be the case. It seems probable that the king brought masons from Normandy to build it. The church was cruciform, with aisles to the nave and presbytery, which had two bays and an apse. The side aisles were also terminated by apses. Over the crossing was a high tower. The aisles were vaulted. At the west end was a 'vestibule'. The Abbey Church at Jumièges had been begun in 1040. In its turn it had followed the type of the church at Bernay, begun about 1020. This fine early church, in a little town half-way between Rouen and Caen . . . is a most important monument for the history of northern architecture. It is cruciform, and had three apses, which are destroyed.

Clapham, in the book already mentioned, confirms Lethaby's view that the immediate ancestry of our English Norman churches is to be found at Bernay and Jumièges. He goes a stage further back by explaining that the beginnings of Norman architecture in its homeland may be traced to the monastic revival instigated by the Italian St. William of Volpiano, Abbot of S. Bénigne at Dijon,

who was summoned to Normandy in 1002 by Duke Richard II to reform the monastic life of the Duchy. With him came a colony of Benedictines from Dijon, who were settled at Fécamp. Jumièges also came under his influence and Bernay was founded under his auspices. In spite of these historical connexions with Burgundy and Italy, there is little or no trace of southern influence in the subsequent architecture of Normandy, though the plan of Jumièges was 'no doubt derived from the adjoining provinces on the south'.

Edward the Confessor's great church of Westminster Abbey is depicted in the Bayeux Tapestry, with a nave of six bays, a short chancel, and a lofty central tower—buttressed by angle turrets—over the crossing; but the primitive drawing—or rather stitchery—leaves a good deal to the imagination. Nothing of the church itself remains to-day except some foundations showing that it occupied the site of the present structure; but a substantial section of the conventual buildings may still be seen, the upper storey being occupied partly by the library and partly by Westminster School. The lower storey is a long vaulted building with a row of sturdy columns down the centre. This building includes the so-called 'Chapel of the Pyx'.

The important fact about this great church, erected *before* the Conquest but under Norman influence, is that it revolutionized the whole science and art of architecture in England. Less than a century later, William of Malmesbury wrote that it was 'now emulated by nearly all in sumptuous outlay.' . . . 'Now you may see in villages churches, in towns monasteries, rise in the new style of building.' Yet though Edward the Confessor changed the fashion of building the greater churches so radically, it was left to the Conqueror to spread the movement over our land.

No sooner were the Normans established here [writes Sir Thomas Jackson] than they began to pull down the existing churches and rebuild them on a more magnificent scale: most of the Saxon churches only dated from the time of Canute, and could not have fallen into disrepair in so short a time, for the Saxon masonry is on

the whole as good as, if not better than, that of the
Normans, much of which is very bad. The general
rebuilding was dictated by the ambition of impressing
themselves visibly on the conquered soil, and leaving
behind them an unmistakeable mark of their superiority
to the conquered race in art as well as in arms. The
Saxon buildings were small compared with those the
conquerors had left behind them in Normandy. But they
were not content to build here as they built there: their
work on the conquered soil should be still vaster and
grander.

(There is a touch of the Hitler spirit in this conception
of the victor imposing his cultural ideas upon a vanquished nation.) When one considers that the total
population of our country is estimated by modern
historians at something between $1\frac{1}{4}$ and $1\frac{1}{2}$ millions at
the time of Domesday (1086), the magnitude of the
Norman achievement can be realized, for it included a
vast amount of castle-building as well as churches,
though domestic architecture at this period was relatively
negligible (p. 82).

Among the immense number of large Saxon churches
rebuilt during the last third of the eleventh century, the
cathedrals of Canterbury, Lincoln, and Durham, and
the great abbey-churches of St. Albans and Ely, assumed
the three-apse form used at Westminster, but all were
subsequently remodelled. The principal examples with
an ambulatory or aisle round the main apse were
the cathedrals of Winchester (begun 1079), Worcester
(1084), Chichester (*c.* 1095), Norwich (1096); and the
great abbey-churches of Gloucester, Tewkesbury, and
St. Augustine at Canterbury. The chief surviving contemporary examples in Normandy are the abbeys of La
Trinité (1062–6) and St. Étienne (1064–73) at Caen,

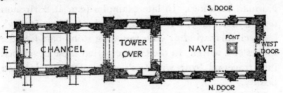

20. IFFLEY CHURCH, NEAR OXFORD
(*above*) West End; (*below*) Plan

commonly known as the 'Abbaye-aux-Dames' and the 'Abbaye-aux-Hommes' respectively; St. Nicholas at Caen (begun *c.* 1083); and the abbeys of Cerisy-la-Forêt, Montivilliers, and Lessay.

One characteristic feature, the round arch, appears in Norman buildings of all shapes and sizes. It need hardly be repeated that it was an inheritance from Roman architecture, and that it had been used by Saxon builders long before the Conquest. It is equally the distinctive feature of Romanesque architecture in all Continental Europe, and the stage at which it gave place to the pointed arch generally marks the transition to the Gothic style in the second half of the twelfth century. In foreign examples, especially in northern Italy and the Rhineland, it is also used decoratively outside and inside buildings in the form of arcading: to a less extent this arcading is found in England (Fig. 23). The illustration of the small but very beautiful church at Iffley near Oxford (Fig. 20) gives an excellent idea of the effect of round arches over doors and windows, and here there is a 'blind' arch (i.e. blocked with masonry) on either side of the central doorway; also a row of very small arches near the top of the tower, the battlements of which are a late Gothic addition. Over the central doorway is a circular window, a less common feature of Norman buildings. In late examples (e.g. at Barfreston near Canterbury), we sometimes find a 'wheel window', i.e. a circular window with radiating stone bars like the spokes of a wheel. In the Gothic period these developed into traceried 'rose windows', often of great size and beauty.

The jambs or sides of the doorways, and sometimes also of the windows, were recessed, as at Iffley, in a

series of square recesses, some of which contained small stone pillars or shafts, each with a capital and base; others were decorated with crude grotesque ornaments, such as the chevron or zigzag, or the beak-head type, both used at Iffley. Floral decoration was also used, and may be seen in the charming doorway of the small church at Kilpeck in Herefordshire (Fig. 21). The tympanum or semicircular space over the lintel of the door—as at Kilpeck—was often carved with some

21. KILPECK CHURCH,
HEREFORDSHIRE

religious subject. It is most confusing to a student that the recesses just described are technically described as 'orders', though they have no relation whatever to the familiar Orders of Greek and Roman architecture.

The church at Iffley is of very simple plan, with a nave only 20 feet wide and a chancel only 16 feet wide, but the total length externally is 114 feet. There is a sturdy central tower, a fairly steep timber roof, and no aisles. The roof is carried on the massive walls without the use of arches between nave and aisles as found in the larger churches (Fig. 23). Such arches were invariably round, supported on very massive cylindrical or polygonal piers. The cylindrical piers at Durham and Gloucester Cathedrals are of enormous diameter, in the former

case decorated with diagonal fluting and zigzag chan-
nellings.

The roofs of nearly all the smaller churches, and for
many years those of the main nave and choir of the
larger churches too, were constructed with timber
trusses and covered with lead or shingles. Usually the
roof was left open and visible internally, but sometimes
there was a flat wooden ceiling, boarded and painted in
geometrical patterns as at Peterborough Cathedral.

The frequency with which churches were destroyed by
fire led to experiments with stone vaulting. At first, this
was confined to the relatively narrow aisles (Fig. 23),
because the immense weight of the heavy stone vault
exercised a great outward thrust upon the supporting
walls, and the builders dared not face the risk of attempt-
ing to span the much wider nave with a thick stone
vault which would obviously cause a proportionately
greater thrust upon much higher walls: the higher a wall
the more easily is it overturned by an outward thrust at
or near its top. Fig. 23 shows a large church with the
nave covered by a wooden roof while the aisles are
vaulted in stone. Each truss or frame of the roof rests
on a pier of the nave arcade, and opposite each truss the
outward wall is strengthened by a flat buttress: this is
the germ of the much more scientific Gothic construction
which was to follow, when piers and buttresses were
designed to carry all the weight of the roof, and the
thickness of the wall between buttresses was reduced to
a minimum.

The first type of vault used in England was the barrel-
vault or tunnel-vault as may be seen in the chapel of the
'White Tower' of the Tower of London (c. 1080), where
the tiny nave is only 14 feet wide and the walls enor-

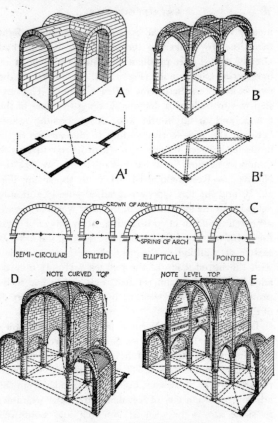

22. DIAGRAMS OF VAULTING

A, Intersecting barrel-vaults; B, Romanesque ribbed vault;
A¹ and B¹, perspective plans of A and B; C, Vaulting arches;
D, Romanesque sexpartite vault; E, Gothic vault (early
period).

Note: for the sake of clearness, windows and buttresses are
omitted, but see Fig. 17.

mously thick. But the aisles required windows to light them, thereby weakening the walls. The Romans had already solved this problem by using cross-vaults or intersecting barrel-vaults (Fig. 22, A) the line where the two vaults intersected being called a 'groin'. The next step was to build ribs diagonally along the lines of the groins, and to fill in the webs or intervening spaces between the ribs—corresponding to the surface of an umbrella between its steel ribs—with lighter stonework than was needed for a barrel-vault: thus we get the Norman or Romanesque ribbed vault shown in Fig. 22, B, and, as this type was gradually and cautiously extended to the loftier nave, in the later Norman period, we reach the form of construction shown in 22, D. At this point we may defer further discussion of the difficult matter of vaulting to the next chapter, in connexion with the introduction of the pointed arch. It may be added that, in England, vaulted roofs always had to be protected against the weather by steeply pitched roofs of timber above them.

Towers during the Norman period, of which Iffley furnishes a small example, were usually placed over the 'crossing' in the larger churches (Fig. 23), and many of them have since collapsed. There is a splendid specimen of early date at St. Albans, built of bricks rifled from the adjoining Roman city of Verulamium. Later examples in stone are to be seen at Norwich and Southwell Cathedrals and at Tewkesbury Abbey; all are freely decorated with stone arcading. There are also twin western towers at Durham, Southwell, and Lincoln Cathedrals and Worksop Priory; and twin towers over the transepts at Exeter Cathedral. The original roofs or spires of all these towers have perished, but it seems probable that the pyramidal form adopted at Southwell, when the old towers were rebuilt in 1711, is a correct reproduction, and this type naturally led to the loftier Gothic spires of the next period. Round towers have survived in many parish-churches of East Anglia.

The interior of the greater Norman churches, as of some small ones, was often decorated with geometrical and floral patterns in crude primary colours, painted on the plastered rubble walls. This type of ornament was largely copied in churches and chapels of all denominations during the Gothic Revival of the nineteenth century (p. 180), and is often more archaeologically correct than pleasing to the eye. The geometrical patterns painted on the wooden ceiling of Peterborough Cathedral have been compared to an Eastern carpet or rug. At St. Albans are some large didactic wall-paintings of figure-subjects. Stained glass had been used in Europe and the East, both by Muslims and by Christians, long before the Norman Conquest; but the earliest known examples surviving in this country are later than the Norman period proper, and are at the Cathedrals of York (1170) and Canterbury (1185–90).

The large church illustrated in Fig. 23 is imaginary, because not a single important example in England retains its Norman form unaltered; and it is drawn with its west end removed to show the construction, a method of presentation much used by the French architectural writer Choisy and often employed by more recent authorities. Some later diagrams in this book follow the same precedent. The plan shows the normal lay-out of the greater churches, whether monastic or otherwise, with three apses at the east end, and three altars in each transept in addition to the high altar at the east end.

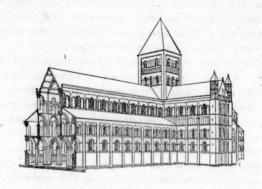

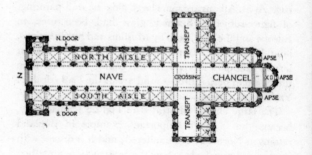

23. A TYPICAL NORMAN CATHEDRAL
(*above*) Sectional View; (*below*) Ground Plan

The altar, not the pulpit, was the important feature in the medieval church. The nave was usually much longer than the choir, the west end was somewhat wider than the nave, and there was a single transept. But this plan, seen to perfection at Peterborough, was by no means universal. Mention has already been made of the 'ambulatory plan', used at Norwich Cathedral (1096–1119), where there are also three radiating chapels projecting from the ambulatory. In French cathedrals there is often a complete chain of such chapels round the east end, forming a 'chevet'. When Canterbury Cathedral was rebuilt and its chancel greatly lengthened in the twelfth century, the original triple apse gave place to the ambulatory. A third type of plan had a square east end, without apses, many large churches being rebuilt in that form during the century.

Circular or 'centrally planned' churches, modelled on the Church of the Holy Sepulchre at Jerusalem as a result of the early Crusades, were often dedicated to St. Sepulchre. Many have been destroyed, and now the chief Norman examples are at Cambridge and Northampton.

Externally and structurally, there was no difference between monastic and other churches, though the ritual arrangements internally were not the same. Of modern cathedrals, the following were originally monastic churches: Ely, Chester, Durham, Gloucester, Winchester, St. Albans, Canterbury, Rochester, Norwich, Peterborough, Bath, Bury St. Edmunds, and Worcester (all Benedictine) ; Carlisle, Southwark, Oxford (all Augustinian). It will thus be seen that the Benedictine order of monks, which drew its inspiration largely from Normandy, was the most active force in English church-building immediately after the Conquest. The Cluniacs who followed exerted much less influence in this country, but the Cistercians who arrived from France in 1128 carried out a great programme which included a number of important abbeys, especially in Yorkshire, e.g. at Fountains (c. 1135) and Kirkstall (1155–60). The Cistercians were architectural puritans who objected to 'the immoderate length, superfluous breadth, costly polishing, and strange designs' of the Benedictines: their churches were, at first, very plain and devoid of ornament. Towers were prohibited, and neither wall-paintings nor stained glass windows were permitted. The subsidiary buildings of the monastery—chapter-house, refectory, dormitory, kitchen, infirmary, abbot's lodging, guest-house for travellers, etc.—and the cloister around which some of them were always grouped, usually on the south side of the church, are of absorbing interest ; but their architectural features and their construction followed those of the churches, and the necessarily limited scope of this little book precludes any description of them here.

The same restriction applies to the notable castles of the Normans, likewise of great interest, but military architecture as such must also be omitted from our consideration, though in the next chapter the gradual transition from the fortified dwelling to the semi-fortified or unfortified manor-house is briefly described (p. 104). As for the dwellings of the ordinary folk in the eleventh and twelfth centuries, hardly any of these survive, and it may safely be assumed that the mass of the people lived under conditions of great discomfort in primitive houses of wood covered with thatch. The so-called 'Jew's House' at Lincoln is almost the only exception known to me. It is substantially built of stone, and its architectural features are characteristic of the Norman period, but it has been much altered.

In Victorian days it was rashly assumed that all the churches of the Middle Ages (presumably including parish-churches) were somehow designed and built by monks or by architects trained in monastic schools. This view, now generally discredited, seems to have originated from a passage in Montalembert's *Les Moines d'Occident* (1877):

When we say that the innumerable monastic churches scattered over the face of all Europe were built by the monks, this statement must be accepted in its literal sense. They were, in fact, not only the architects, but even the masons of their buildings; having drawn up their plans, of which the noble and skilful design still arouses our admiration, they carried them out with their own hands, and, as a general rule, without the assistance of workmen from outside. They chanted psalms as they worked, and laid down their tools only to go to the altar or the choir. They undertook the most arduous tasks, and exposed themselves to all the fatigue and danger of the mason's craft. The abbots themselves were not content with drawing plans and supervising the work; they gave personally an example of courage and humility, and shrank from no weary labour. While simple monks were often the chief architects of the buildings, the abbots willingly condescended to act as common workmen.

Modern scholarship, led by the learned Dr. Coulton, contradicts every single statement in this imaginative paragraph, and maintains that both design and construction were almost exclusively the work of hired laymen, throughout the Middle Ages. This compels me to retract the moderate opinion expressed in my book *The Architect in History* (1927), that the control of building passed from clerical to lay hands in the mid-twelfth century; and to extend to the early Norman period my considered views on architects and builders in the later Middle Ages, as summarized on pp. 105, 117–19 of the present volume.

Norman architecture lacks the emotional and intellectual appeal of Gothic, where every stone seems to be pulling its weight and singing a song the while; but it displays qualities of dignity and immense strength, especially in the larger cathedrals and abbeys.

CHAPTER 7

EARLY GOTHIC ARCHITECTURE IN ENGLAND (*c.* 1150–1350)

THE WORD 'Gothic' has so long been associated in the English mind with the noblest architectural monuments of our country that we are apt to forget that it was originally applied as a nickname or term of abuse or reproach, comparable with 'Whig' or 'Tory' or 'Quaker'. It first occurs in print about 1663 to describe what John Evelyn called 'congestions of heavy, dark, melancholy and monkish piles, without any just proportion, use or beauty'—such as Westminster Abbey—and its origin may be explained by a couplet of Dryden's:

> Till Goths and Vandals, a rude northern race,
> Did all the matchless monuments deface.

The Goths, it may be recalled, were a Germanic tribe who invaded the civilized countries of Europe between the third and fifth centuries, and the Vandals were another Germanic tribe who followed them. It is a historical fact that both these tribes did destroy many of the magnificent cities and buildings of the Romans; so that, 'by transference', as the dictionary says, a 'Goth' or a 'Vandal' is 'one who behaves like a barbarian, especially in the destruction or neglect of works of art'. Yet, while we still use both these epithets in that sense, we accept 'Gothic' nowadays without cavil, because the nickname has lost all its sting since it was first invented nearly three hundred years ago.

As will be explained in Chapter 12, there came a time when dilettante interest, and later popular interest, was focused on medieval architecture after some two centuries of utter neglect. As the study of these forgotten masterpieces developed, it soon called for a system of classification and nomenclature almost as precise and pedantic as that of the classical Orders. Everything had to be labelled. The pioneers in this field were Thomas Rickman, not an architect or a Churchman but an archaeologically-minded Quaker, who in 1817 published *An Attempt to discriminate the Styles of Architecture in England, from the Conquest to the Reformation*; and Edmund Sharpe the architect, whose *Seven Periods of English Architecture* appeared in 1851. Rickman adopted or invented the terms 'Norman', 'Early English', 'Decorated', and 'Perpendicular'; and the 'Transitional' periods which intervened between them. They held the field till recent times, when the fashion for disparaging every product of 'eminent Victorians' led to a tendency to discard terms which had become somewhat hackneyed and were not entirely satisfactory. 'Norman' now tends to become 'English Romanesque' (cf. p. 67); 'Early English' is replaced by 'Early Pointed' or 'Lancet'; 'Decorated' is described as 'Middle Pointed' or subdivided into 'Geometrical' and 'Curvilinear'; 'Perpendicular' becomes 'Rectilinear' or 'Late Pointed'; and 'Tudor' is added to the list. Finally, the arbitrary dating of periods is abolished, and architecture is classified by centuries.

If we can forgo the temptation to sneer at everything our grandfathers did, and view the matter impartially, it will be found that Rickman's periods were, in fact, very accurately defined: they did indicate the chief stages of architectural development, viz.: Norman 1066–

1189; Early English 1189–1307; Decorated 1307–77; Perpendicular 1377–1546; with Transitional periods 1189–99, 1272–1307, 1327–77—the reigns of kings being used as a basis. Obviously Rickman never intended that this approximate classification should be regarded literally: e.g. that every building erected in any part of England in, say, 1189, must be Norman; and it is just because he did not and could not determine the points of change to a precise year that he took the reigns of kings as an approximate basis. Classification by centuries utterly fails if applied to Gothic architecture: in so far as any lines can be drawn between the various periods, they occur at *about* 1150, 1250, 1350, and 1550. For the purpose of this little book, it is convenient to divide all Gothic architecture proper (i.e. post-Norman and pre-Renaissance, say 1150–1550) into two simple categories: 'Early Gothic' to *c.* 1350, 'Late Gothic' after *c.* 1350, the Black Death of 1348–50 forming roughly the dividing line. Thus each stage covers approximately 200 years.

Whatever system of classification be adopted, it must be remembered that the change from one 'period' or 'style' to the next was always gradual and never abrupt. Some ingenious or enterprising architect or mason or carpenter had a bright idea, tried it on one building, and then waited to see what happened. Sometimes the result was disastrous : cracks developed, a central tower or a vault collapsed, and there was loss of life. Sometimes all went well, and the idea was adopted elsewhere, taking years to reach the remoter parts of England, if indeed it penetrated there within a generation. Thus the 'Transition' from the mature Norman or English-Romanesque architecture of the nave of Norwich

Cathedral (finished before 1145) and the completely 'Early English' Gothic of the choir of Lincoln Cathedral (begun 1192) is a most difficult process to trace. In brief, the change consisted in the introduction of the pointed arch: at first into the arcades of the nave and choir, then into vaulting of the greater churches, and finally for doors and windows and every other part of a building where semi-circular arches had previously been used. Other changes, such as the development of buttressing and the thinning of walls between buttresses, followed as part of the improvement in vaulting, while many fresh ornamental forms were introduced which had no constructional significance.

The pointed arch seems to have been brought into England by the Cistercians (p. 82) when they arrived in 1128 from Burgundy, where it was already in common use; and the oldest surviving example in this country occurs in the nave-arcade of Fountains Abbey (c. 1135). There, as in the other early Cistercian abbeys of Kirkstall (c. 1155) and Buildwas (c. 1155), pointed arches are employed for the nave-arcade while semicircular arches continue to be used for doors and windows. In the royal domain of the Île-de-France, the cathedrals of St. Denis (consecrated 1140) and Senlis (1154) already display most of the distinctive characteristics of Gothic design and construction. So does the cathedral of Sens, in Burgundy (1143–68), and when Master William, its architect, had completed his work there, he was brought over to England to rebuild the choir of Canterbury Cathedral, burned down in 1174; and remained in charge for four years, until he had a fall from the scaffold, and had to retire to France in 1179, severely injured.

Thus we find that the pointed arch, used for so many

centuries in the Mediterranean and Middle Eastern
countries (pp. 56-8), was first introduced into our own
land from France by Cistercian monks in 1135, long
before Gothic construction was developed in this country;
and that French architects had made the change from
Romanesque to Gothic many years before we did. We
cannot deny our debt to France in that respect, though
within two generations later England produced a style
of architecture—commonly called 'Early English'—
which was distinctively national and of which Salisbury
Cathedral (Figs. 24-25) is perhaps the most typical
example.

   Gothic architecture spread all over western and central
Europe, as Romanesque architecture had done previously. It is found not only in France and England,
but in Germany, Spain, Portugal, Belgium, Holland,
Switzerland, Scandinavia, Italy, Czechoslovakia, the
Dalmatian coast, parts of Poland, and it even penetrated
to Palestine and Cyprus in the wake of the Crusaders. In
fact it occurs in all countries which the Roman Catholic
Church dominated in the Middle Ages, but not in Russia
or the Balkan countries where the Greek Church prevailed. In Italy, whatever Ruskin says, it was never
wholly acclimatized; for the classical tradition persisted
everywhere, and the first dawn of the Renaissance was
welcomed there whole-heartedly a century or more
before it had made any impression on the rest of Europe,
and two centuries before the Gothic tradition was
finally smothered in England. But all the other countries
mentioned above drew their inspiration from France,
and the cathedrals of Germany and Spain are only
rather inferior specimens of French Gothic. Thus the
first architect of the Cathedral at Prague was a French-

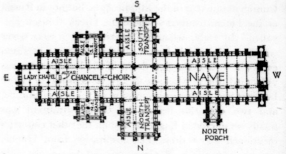

24. SALISBURY CATHEDRAL
(*above*) View from N.W.; (*below*) Ground Plan

man, as were those of the chief early Gothic cathedrals in Spain.

In France, three great Gothic cathedrals soon followed St. Denis: viz. Notre Dame at Paris, mostly built 1163–96 and completed after a short interval in 1218–23; Chartres, mostly rebuilt 1194–1212; and Laon, 1160–1205. A few years later came another great galaxy: Amiens, 1220–69; Bourges, early thirteenth century; Beauvais, begun 1247 but never completed; and Reims, begun 1211 but not finished till the end of the fourteenth century. In England the chief Gothic cathedrals are slightly later in date; viz. Lincoln choir and apse begun 1192, nave c. 1209–35, 'Angel Choir' 1255–80; Salisbury 1220–66; Wells west front 1220–39; York transepts 1230–60, nave 1291–1324; and with these may be mentioned Westminster Abbey, choir and transepts 1245–69, nave later though in much the same style.

Before considering Gothic architecture in detail, and comparing English with French characteristics, we may turn to Lethaby's inspired pages for his views on Gothic as a whole, which he describes as 'probably the most original of all theories of building'. He continues:

It is impossible to explain in words the content of perfect Gothic art. It is frank, clear, gay; it is passionate, mystical and tender; it is energetic, sharp, strong and healthy. It was born of the land and the people—a folk art. To try to define it in terms of form alone would be a mistake; it embodied a spirit, an aspiration, an age. The ideals of the time of energy and order produced a manner of building of high intensity; all waste tissue was thrown off, and the stonework was gathered up into energetic functional members. These rods and bars and shafts are all at bowstring tension. A mason will tap a pillar to make its stress audible; we may think of a cathedral as so 'high strung' that if struck it would give a musical note. . . .

Churches of the first class in the thirteenth century were built to be covered by stone vaults, which vaults were membered—that is, made up of stronger supporting ribs and thinner webs filling spaces between them; each 'bay' or compartment being a sort of stone pavilion. These radiating ribs gathered up the weight and thrusts at given points above tall and slender supports. The planning was thus the resultant of a sum of several exigencies. The ritual gave one condition, the size another, the necessities of vaulted construction a third, and so on. Now, especially in a stone-covered church, the width may not be increased too recklessly, whereas the addition of length is easy. Yet obviously an interior may not be drawn out into too long a tunnel. Lateral annexes may, however, be added, especially opposite a central point, and such 'transepts' not only increase the volume of a building, but, standing in opposition to the long central vault, they form supports to it. . . .

Up to a point in architectural history, the planning of great churches was a matter of experiment, of adjustment and development within narrow boundaries, and the solution found was practical, geometrical and traditional. . . . The medieval builders, when they had found their theory of construction, did not, like the Roman architects, lock up their arches in great masses of masonry, but they set arch to fight arch; until two, four, eight or a dozen were balanced on one slender pier. They cross like the jets from a fountain, and spread like the branches of great trees so that old writers thought that the architecture had been suggested by avenues in a wood.

The branching arches of the high vault were constantly exercising an expanding pressure against the walls of the clerestory, which themselves were suspended above the tall arcades of the interior. To counterbalance this, other arches were built in the open air, reaching up from the low side walls of the outer aisles and forming props to the central span. These flying buttresses, as they have been well called, were surely an extraordinary invention. In many French churches, there are two tiers of these, which spring from tall, heavy pinnacles. The design of the superstructure of a great church was conceived as a problem in equilibrium. The builders made an effort to do all that might be done in stone, and the possibilities of rearing stones one upon another were explored to the utmost. The structure, as Morris has well put it, became organic. This was the law of growth in Gothic architecture. . . .

The essence of a Gothic cathedral is its structure, not its adornments, though never so beautiful. . . . The cathedral had much wealth of sculptures, paintings, stained glass, embroideries, gold and silver treasure. These things, it is true, were a part of the means of teaching, of ritual and folk tradition, but they do not make up the essential cathedral. In one sense they were merely superadded, like the music and the incense; in another, it is true, they themselves furnished real data to the builders. Thus a cathedral, in one aspect, was a stone shrine made with enamels of storied glass; in another it had to provide great stone avenues for stately processions, in which the whispering and wailing organs might speak, and the cloud of incense might ascend. . . . The fairy architecture, the glory of the stained glass, the might of the bells, the sweet incense, the organ music, and the splendour of the altars and vestments, all contributed to the most marvellous of all dramas—medieval worship.

These lengthy and glowing quotations are taken from the chapter on 'French Gothic' in Professor Lethaby's *Architecture* (pp. 191–9), and they serve to describe the spirit of Gothic in general. He says very little about the features which differentiate French Gothic from English, which he regards as 'an offshoot from the parent stock of France', and he is chiefly concerned with the cathedrals and greater churches. If we confine ourselves, for the

moment, to those buildings, we find that, in general,
English Gothic cathedrals are narrower, longer, and
lower than the French examples. Whereas, in France, the
Norman apse developed into a chevet (p. 81), in England
it came to be replaced by a square east end, Westminster
Abbey being a rare exception where the French chevet
is found. In France, cloisters are seldom found adjoining
cathedrals, but in England they are common, because
so many of the English cathedrals were originally built
as monastic churches. In France, transepts were shallow,
in England deep, and sometimes duplicated, as at Salisbury, Lincoln, and Worcester. The breadth of French
cathedrals is due to the frequent use of double aisles and
side chapels between each pair of buttresses, whereas in
England single aisles without side chapels are generally
found. As for towers, French practice favoured two
western towers, sometimes with a magnificent *fléche* over
the crossing, as at Notre Dame, Paris; but as many as
seven or even nine towers are occasionally found. In
England the lofty and massive central tower is preferred,
with or without western towers, and three towers are a
maximum. On the whole, the interior architecture
(apart from ornament) of English cathedrals is more
elaborate than that of France.

We must now proceed to consider the effect that the
pointed arch—the dominant feature of Gothic architecture—had upon building. Pointed arches were not
introduced into England because they pointed to
Heaven, or because they were considered intrinsically
beautiful. They are, in fact, somewhat stronger than the
semicircular type so long as they retain a pure pointed
form; and in several respects they are more conveniently
handled in constructional design than the Norman form.

Their introduction into vaulting enabled the twelfth-century builders to solve some of the difficult problems that had been troubling them for many years. As we have already seen (p. 78), the Normans abandoned the use of heavy barrel-vaults over the aisles of their larger churches, substituting for them ribbed groined vaults as illustrated in Fig. 22, B. The use of ribs proved such a success in producing an economical stone roof that they naturally began to experiment with fireproof vaults over the wider span of the nave. Referring to Fig. 22, A and B, we see that the early groined vaults, whether with or without ribs, have arches of the same size, and that all these arches are semicircular. So it appears, but obviously if the transverse and wall arches in B are semicircular and of equal span, the diagonal rib must have a greater span; hence, it must either rise to a higher point or lose its semicircular form, becoming elliptical or segmental. The English builders liked to keep the tops ('crowns') of their vaults, as well as the points from which they sprang at the base, level throughout; and, as they had not yet discovered the pointed arch, they distorted the diagonal arches into segmental or elliptical form. Now this was all very well in the aisles, but when they came to deal with the wide vault over the nave, they found it necessary, for purposes of strength and to enable them to relate the nave vault to the vaulting system of the aisles, to have two arches in the nave arcade and two bays of aisle vaulting for every square bay of the nave vault. Therefore the arch of the nave vault would be twice as wide as the arches of the nave arcade, but much less wide than the diagonal rib; and hence, if all the arches had been made semicircular, and had 'sprung' from the same level at their bases, their tops would have been at three very different heights, and the effect would have been unsatisfactory. So the builders got out of their difficulty once more by distorting the arches, as Fig. 22, C explains. For the nave they employed a proper semicircular arch, for the longer diagonal rib a segmental arch of similar height but of depressed curve, and for the narrow wall-arches a 'stilted' arch of the same height. Each bay of a vault like 22, D has six parts, and hence is known as a 'sexpartite' vault.

The concern of the builders with the shape of their vaulting ribs has been explained partly to show the great importance of the introduction of the pointed arch at the end of the Norman period; for Fig. 22, C indicates that the width of a pointed arch can be varied a considerable amount while its height remains constant. Thus it solved all the vaulting difficulties: the wall-arches could be narrow and sharply pointed, the transverse rib across the nave could be twice as wide and more bluntly pointed, and the diagonal rib—perhaps half as long again—could be a true semicircle. Now all distortion was avoided, and the subsequent progress of Gothic vaulting consisted of a continual striving to lighten all parts of the structure, so that thin webs of cut stones—only 6 inches or so thick—filled the spaces between vaulting ribs of moulded masonry, themselves reduced to the slightest possible dimensions. If you compare the construction of the early Gothic cathedral at Salisbury (Fig. 25) with that of the late Gothic chapel at King's College, Cambridge (Fig. 29), you will readily trace the progressive lightening of the structure.

One result of the concentration of the weight of the roof, whether by stone vaulting ribs or by wooden trusses, on to certain points in the wall was that the wall needed

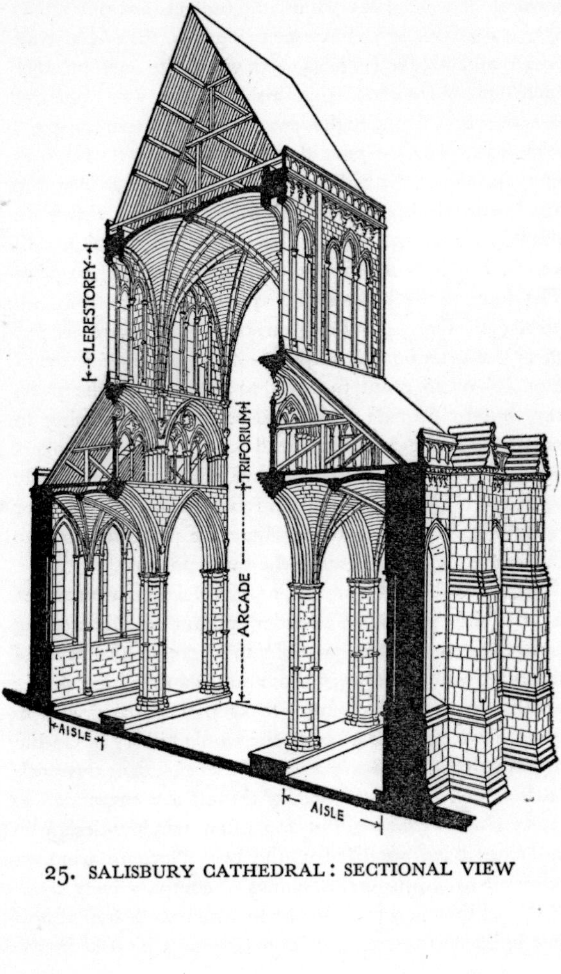
CLERESTOREY
TRIFORIUM
ARCADE
AISLE
AISLE

25. SALISBURY CATHEDRAL: SECTIONAL VIEW

strengthening at those points. So buttresses were added, at first very flat as we have seen (Fig. 23), then becoming larger and bolder (Fig. 25). It was quite easy to erect these massive buttresses against the aisle wall, but the strengthening of the high clerestory wall, where the great stone vault over the nave threatened to push it over, was more difficult. At Salisbury there is an arch over the aisle vault (hidden by the aisle roof but just visible on the left of Fig. 25) which helps to support the high wall above, but it is not in the best place for the purpose. The tops of the buttresses frequently terminate in tall pinnacles (Fig. 24). These striking features are *not* put there for ornamental purposes—though they are ornamental—or to point the way to Heaven, as the poets say, but to provide additional strength by helping to press down the buttresses and keep them from overturning. Their pyramidal tops are so fashioned primarily to throw off water, and the carefully designed slopes or 'weatherings' at each stage where the projection of the buttress is diminished serve the same purpose.

As the vault was lightened, and its weight concentrated at definite points on slender pillars and projecting buttresses, it became possible to decrease the area of masonry walling between those points and to increase the area of glass. It is essential to keep this fact clearly in mind, for it supplies a key to the whole history of Gothic architecture. *The development of the window design was only made possible because the thrust of the roof was concentrated on to piers and buttresses:* but too often window-design in itself has been regarded as the key. Norman windows were all round-headed openings of comparatively small size, and they had to be so, for the thick walls had almost negligible buttresses, and large openings pierced in the walls at frequent intervals would have seriously diminished their strength. Now refer to Figs. 24–25, illustrating Salisbury Cathedral, the typical great English church of the thirteenth century. Buttresses have been introduced, so it is possible now to provide a much larger area of glass. In the aisle wall there is a pair of plain 'lancet' windows with pointed heads between each pair of buttresses; in the high clerestory wall there is a triplet of lancet windows, a development of the Norman triplet

26A. EARLY GOTHIC
CAPITAL: LINCOLN

26B. MID-GOTHIC
CAPITAL: SOUTHWELL

shown in Fig. 23. The pair in the aisle, like the triplet in the clerestory, are connected by a 'dripmould' or 'dripstone' (the mould above their heads to throw off the rain running down the face of the wall) and thus form a group. In fact, the triplet in the clerestory, with only thin pillars of stone between the separate windows or 'lights', does definitely suggest a single window.

By this time, the art of glass-painting was beginning to develop too, but most of the thirteenth-century windows are glazed with a beautiful 'grisaille' (greenish-grey) glass such as one sees in the famous 'Five Sisters'

at York Minster. Partly to give more light, partly to
provide a field for the glass-painter's art, the increase of
window-area now continued (see Fig. 28). Two or three
lancet windows were grouped together under one enclosing arch and dripstone in a thin portion of the wall,
a mere 'plate' of stone, and the blank part of the plate between the heads of the lancets was pierced with circular

27. WINCHELSEA CHURCH: EAST END

or trefoil or quatrefoil or cinquefoil lights (Fig. 28, A).
This is called 'plate-tracery'. Next the pillars of stone
were reduced to still smaller dimensions, and the shafts
that had hitherto been built in front of them were
omitted, so that only a mullion of stone perhaps 6 inches
wide and a foot deep, separated the lights. The mullion
was 'chamfered' off or moulded so that it obstructed as
little light as possible, and the edge of the mullion both
inside and outside the window is usually only an inch

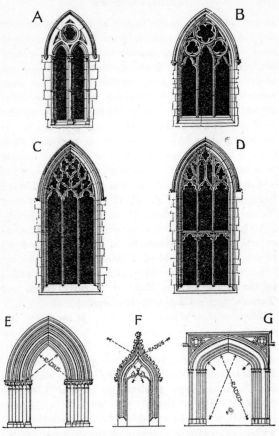

28. GOTHIC WINDOWS AND DOORWAYS

A, Plate tracery; B, Geometrical tracery; C, Curvilinear tracery; D, Rectilinear tracery with transome; E, Acutely pointed arch; F. Ogee arch; G, Four-centred or 'Tudor' arch.

or two wide. The jambs (sides) of the windows were similarly splayed to allow as much light as possible to enter. The next step was to reduce the stonework between the lancet-heads and the other pierced openings to the same thickness as the mullions, so that the stone 'tracery' seemed to wind round the geometrical openings of the window-head from its springing point on the mullions. This is 'Geometrical' tracery (Fig. 28, B). As the skill and ambition of the masons increased, their fancy led them to twist this tracery into more flowing lines, no longer limited by the strict geometrical forms of earlier days, and 'Curvilinear' tracery was evolved in the fourteenth century (Fig. 28, C). Meanwhile a new feature has been introduced: the heads of the lancet-lights have been 'foliated' or 'cusped', as well as the ornamental piercings between them. Foliated or cusped arches originated in Muslim buildings as early as the ninth century, perhaps earlier, and they are to be added to the many features that we borrowed from our 'Saracen' foes in Cairo and elsewhere.

The evolution of Gothic doorways is much less important than that of windows. Fig. 28, E illustrates an early Gothic example with a sharply pointed or 'acute' arch; and F shows a less common type with an 'ogee' arch of double curvature, which made its appearance in mid-Gothic buildings. It will be noticed that the sloping ('splayed') sides or jambs, of E especially, are deeply moulded, as are also the sides of Gothic windows and arches. A moulding is defined in the dictionary as 'an ornamental variety of contour given to stone-, wood-, or metal-work, effected by means of carving'; but it may consist of carved hollows and rolls, without any ornamental features such as floral bands. In each style and period, from the Greek onwards, such mouldings give refinement and character to buildings; and they are so distinctive that to an expert eye they indicate, in conjunction with the general style of the architecture and the technique of its execution, the approximate date of its erection within limits which Lethaby, rather optimistically, suggests as ten years! Be this as it may, mouldings are important, but in this book it is impossible to treat them in detail. It may be said that early Gothic mouldings are bold and pleasing, and that a characteristic ornamental feature in the thirteenth century was the so-called 'dog-tooth' moulding, consisting of bands of small leaves, arranged in fours to form a pyramid.

During the same century, the characteristic capital consisted of a very beautiful conventional treatment of foliage (Fig. 26, A), on a slender shaft of stone or of dark Purbeck marble, or on a clustered pier. This feature was distinctively English: the French counterpart was a 'Corinthianesque' foliaged capital—a variant of the Corinthian Order previously described, and cylindrical columns were used in nave arcades. As English Gothic developed into the 'Decorated' style of the middle period, the conventional foliage gave place to a naturalistic treatment, seen to perfection in the carved capitals of the chapter-house at Southwell Cathedral (Fig. 26, B, c. 1294), where the carving of plant-forms is so faithful that it seems probable that the carver worked with actual leaves and flowers by his side. Churches of all types were often lavishly decorated internally with paintings on the walls and ceilings or vaults, depicting incidents of the Bible story and of the lives of the saints, sometimes in a most gruesome fashion. This form of decoration was intended primarily to instruct unlettered people in religion, if not indeed to terrify them with pictures of Hell and the tortures of the damned; but it also brightened the churches, and it included a good deal of rather crude geometrical patterning on walls, from which later churches of the nineteenth-century 'Gothic Revival' (p. 180) drew inspiration for better or—more frequently—for worse. At St. Albans Cathedral there are wall-paintings and ceiling-paintings ranging from the thirteenth to the fifteenth century.

Throughout this chapter, the emphasis has been upon cathedrals and the greater monastic churches, many of which became cathedrals at the Reformation or subsequently, up to quite recent times (e.g. St. Albans Abbey became a cathedral in 1878). The architecture of the smaller parish-churches, however, only differed from them in being less ornate and in the fact that stone vaulting was seldom used. As for dwelling-houses, the nobility continued to build castles, and the common people continued to be miserably poor, mostly living in the same sort of huts or shacks as are described in Chapter 6. Nevertheless, a few stone-built houses from the period 1150–1350 still survive, including Markenfield Hall near Ripon (c. 1310); also the so-called 'castles' (really fortified manor-houses) of Oakham and Stokesay (Fig. 30); and Little Wenham Hall in Suffolk is a brick building of the late thirteenth century. In all such secular buildings, the architecture resembles that of the churches; and at Prague in Czechoslovakia there is actually a charming little Jewish synagogue built in pure Gothic style, c. 1316!

Early Gothic figure-sculpture in England, as in France, attained a very high level of excellence; and is to be seen at its best on the west front of Wells Cathedral (1220–39);

but space does not allow of any description of it here. Many critics consider, however, that the richly sculptured west fronts of the cathedrals of Rheims, Chartres, and Paris are far superior as architectural designs to those of Wells and Peterborough, the last-named in particular seeming to have but little relation to the church behind it. An American authority has written of it: 'The design is naïve, daring, illogical. It breathes the spirit of youth, but it is adolescence, not young manhood. It is the awkward age of the Gothic style—all hands and feet and sky-rocketing growth, not the grace and strength of crescent but complete manhood.'

Contrary to popular belief, the names of a large number of medieval architects, even of the early Gothic period, have been preserved; and it is now generally recognized that they were laymen, not clerics. Some of their drawings have survived; and the tomb-slabs of Richard of Gainsborough (d. 1300) at Lincoln Cathedral and of William de Wermington at Croyland Abbey are inscribed with the portraits of those two worthies, while others may be seen in France. A more detailed description of medieval architects and craftsmen, their methods and the conditions under which they worked, will be found at the end of the next chapter.

CHAPTER 8

LATE GOTHIC ARCHITECTURE IN ENGLAND (*c.* 1350–1550)

IT so happens that the date assumed here for the change from 'early' to 'late' Gothic corresponds with that of the Black Death which swept over England in 1348–50, but it is difficult to see how that terrible scourge can have affected the always slow evolution of architectural forms. Lethaby says that it 'cast its shadow over all the arts so that they never recovered their earlier sweetness and elasticity of aspect'; but many people challenge that statement. Professor Trevelyan estimates that the Black Death reduced our population in sixteen months from 'perhaps four million to perhaps two and a half million souls', producing an acute shortage of labour which led to a transference of arable land to sheep-farming, first developed on a large scale by Cistercian monks in the Yorkshire dales. Thus the wool-growing and the weaving counties became wealthier, with the result that many beautiful parish-churches and manor-houses were erected there in late Gothic times, as we shall see. But certain other changes already taking place were accelerated by the shortage of labour and the slow collapse of the feudal system.

The monasteries were at the height of their power in England at the beginning of the early Gothic period, and the majority of the cathedrals built during that period were erected as monastic churches. All through the ensuing two centuries, the hold of the monks on the people was diminishing, although in 1350 they were wealthier than ever. By that time, church-building had largely passed out of their hands, and was confined mainly to 'secular' (i.e. non-monastic) cathedrals and to parish-churches. John Wycliffe's preaching against the laxity, ignorance, and wealth of the monasteries was very popular in the later years of the fourteenth century, and found a receptive soil among the discontented labourers. He was eventually silenced, but his influence persisted and was largely responsible for the Protestant Reformation in England 150 years later. It seems significant, though the point does not appear to have been emphasized before, that the three churches which are usually considered to represent the culmination and final flowering of our Gothic—Henry VII's Chapel at Westminster (1500–12), St. George's Chapel at Windsor (c. 1481–1537), and King's College Chapel at Cambridge (1446–1515)—are all *royal* foundations, testifying to the immense power of the Crown in Henry VII's day and the consequent decline of priestly power. The dissolution of the monasteries in 1536–9 not only marks the end of their long life and the transfer of their wealth to the Crown, but also marks the end of church-building for more than a century. With very few exceptions, no Gothic churches were built from 1540 or so (p. 123) until the combined effects of the Restoration in 1660 and the Great Fire of 1666 led to a revival of church-building under Wren, his new churches being then designed in Renaissance style (p. 155).

'Perpendicular' or 'Rectilinear' architecture, as it is usually called, is peculiar to England. Neither in France nor in other continental countries, which followed French fashions, is there anything corresponding to it. French 'flamboyant' architecture, which suddenly blazed out brilliantly towards the end of the fourteenth century, is so much like the 'Curvilinear' or 'Late Decorated' style which we in England had evolved some seventy years before, that there is justification for inferring that, on this occasion, France was copying England at last; and it may be noted that most of the chief examples of the style are to be found in places such as Rouen, Caudebec, and Abbeville, which were actually under English rule at the time.

The flowing and florid magnificence of the 'Curvilinear' or 'Late Decorated' period in England is best seen in such small examples as the Percy Tomb in Beverley Minster (c. 1340), several tombs in Westminster Abbey of the same era, and the 'Easter Sepulchres' at Hawton in Nottinghamshire, and Heckington in Lincolnshire (the finest Curvilinear church in England); but equal richness is found in the 'Perpendicular' style, and the Black Death certainly did not stifle all exuberance in ornamental detail. It is generally held that the first noteworthy specimen of 'Perpendicular' design is to be seen at Gloucester Cathedral, then a Benedictine abbey and not a cathedral, the choir of which was remodelled by an ambitious abbot in 1337–77. He partly rebuilt the existing Norman structure, and cased the remainder with a veneer of light masonry in the form of tracery to match that of the splendid new windows which replaced the smaller Norman openings. His glorious east window was, and probably still is, the largest in the world, measuring 72 by 38 feet. It is divided by light stone mullions (vertical bars) into fourteen lights and by transomes (horizontal bars) into eight tiers. An ample field was thus provided for the rapidly developing art of

29. KING'S COLLEGE CHAPEL, CAMBRIDGE:
SECTIONAL VIEW SHOWING CONSTRUCTION

30. STOKESAY CASTLE, SHROPSHIRE

the glass-painter. This division of large window areas
into a grid of 'lights' is the characteristic feature of the
style which has earned for it the name of 'Rectilinear'
architecture (see Fig. 28, D). Thus the controlling
element in this phase of building became the window
rather than the more important system of vaulting and
buttressing.

The desire for more light and more painted glass
did lead, however, to further progress in vaulting and
buttressing. The progressive tendency to a reduction
of the thickness of vaulting webs by a multiplication of
stone ribs, a strengthening of buttresses, and a consequent
thinning of walls between buttresses, was accelerated,
and reached its climax in the famous chapel of King's
College at Cambridge (Fig. 29). The illustration shows
that the lofty vaulted roof of filigree stonework is carried
on slender piers of masonry reinforced by enormous
buttresses and capped with tall pinnacles. There are no
aisles to weaken these buttresses, but a chantry chapel
(p. 113) between each pair, and great windows above
each chapel. This triumphant finale of Gothic construction is described by Francis Bond as 'the most
consummate achievement of the masonry of the Middle
Ages, put together with an unerring science and precision
as the parts of a steam-engine or an astronomical
instrument'. The type of vaulting used, as in St.
George's Chapel at Windsor and in Henry VII's Chapel
at Westminster, is 'fan-vaulting', a term easily understood if you refer to Fig. 29; but this was by no means
common in 'Perpendicular' churches, even of the late
period; and 'lierne-vaulting', in which a large number
of intermediate ribs are used, was more normal. As the
illustration shows, a wooden roof, covered with lead,

was required to protect the upper surface of the vault from the weather. Fan-vaulting is peculiar to England, lierne-vaulting is not.

Only the larger churches were vaulted in stone, and English late Gothic architecture surpassed all its foreign cousins in the elaboration and beauty of its open timber roofs, another distinctively English feature. Structurally, the simplest sloping timber roof consists of inclined rafters; but, as they tend to spread apart at their feet, and so overturn the supporting walls, a horizontal tie-beam or 'collar' is inserted to tie their feet together. This method is, however, only adequate for very small roofs of less than 20 feet span. Above that width, 'trusses' (triangular frames of heavy timber) are used. They are spaced at regular intervals, thus dividing the church (or other building) into 'bays' (Fig. 31); and are placed opposite buttresses, as with vaulting, so that the weight of the roof is concentrated at these strengthened points of support and windows of any size can be inserted between them. A simple truss of this kind is shown over the main nave-vault of Salisbury Cathedral in Fig. 25, but the horizontal tie-beam came to be considered unsightly when it was exposed to view, so reliance was placed upon a collar at a much higher level (Fig. 31). Even this did not satisfy the late Gothic builders, who raised the collar still higher and evolved the wonderfully striking but rather unconstructional type known as the 'hammer-beam truss', of which the finest example is the roof over Westminster Hall (1397–9), with the colossal span of 68 feet. Carved angels, heraldry, and wooden 'tracery' were used to enhance the effect of these roofs, and Norfolk contains several fine specimens. In Devon and Somerset we find another most attractive type, the 'wagon roof'; where there is a boarded ceiling under the intersecting rafters, forming a curved surface.

In these late Gothic churches, especially in Devon, Somerset, Norfolk, and Suffolk, there are many magnificent wooden screens, often gaily painted; but purists must find it difficult to justify the imitation in delicate interior woodwork of such typical masonry features as vaulting, buttresses (with weathered tops), pinnacles, tracery, and even battlements!

The characteristic doorway of the late Gothic period has a depressed or 'Tudor' arch (Fig. 28, G), with four 'centres' as shown; and the same type of arch was largely used for windows and sometimes for nave-arcades. Carved ornament of this period is perhaps less attractive and certainly less naturalistic than that of Curvilinear Gothic, but includes much interesting heraldry and a good deal of very competent figure-sculpture. Among the cathedrals and greater churches (besides Gloucester and the three royal chapels previously mentioned), the finest late Gothic examples are the west fronts of Winchester Cathedral and Beverley Minster, the nave and tower of Canterbury, the choir and tower of York, and most of Sherborne Abbey. Smaller examples include Magdalen College Chapel at Oxford with its lovely tower, and the marvellous Beauchamp Chapel at Warwick; but the list might be prolonged indefinitely.

Nevertheless, the period 1350–1550 was still more remarkable for the building (or, more often, rebuilding) of parish-churches. The great majority of these had been founded when Domesday Book was written, and their rebuilding or enlargement coincided with the increased power and popularity of the 'secular' (parish) clergy as compared with the monasteries, and with the growing wealth of certain parts of England, often due to the wool-trade. Indeed, some of the noble churches in the Cotswold district are known as 'wool churches': the same term might be applied equally to many in Norfolk and Suffolk. Visitors to such places as Long Melford and Lavenham are often amazed to find large churches in small villages; but it must be remembered that church attendance for all and sundry was made compulsory in the sixteenth century; yet, even apart from that explanation, some authorities consider that the churches were not too large when they were built. Much of the new floor-space was occupied by chantry chapels, for wealthy men or craft-guilds endowed altars where masses could be said or sung (French *chanter*) in perpetuity, fondly believing that 'works of merit could be posthumously performed'. Thus the general tendency was to widen, lighten, and elaborate the existing structure, whatever measure of rebuilding took place. The plans of parish-churches were usually oblong rather than cruciform, transepts being rare.

In the field of domestic architecture, there was a rapid change during the fifteenth century, but between 1350 and 1400 there is less to record. Doubtless the Black Death was partly responsible for this, but it must not be forgotten that, during the whole period 1350–1550, wars were in progress: in France from 1337 to 1452 (the 'Hundred Years War'), and again intermittently between 1492 and 1557; in England from 1450 to 1485 (the 'Wars of the Roses'). There were also the Peasants' Revolt in 1381 and Cade's insurrection in 1450. One would have thought that all this unrest would have interfered with peaceful house-building, but Professor

31. PENSHURST PLACE, KENT: THE GREAT HALL

Trevelyan considers that it affected social life in England very little, as the 'Wars of the Roses' meant only 'brief occasional campaigns conducted by 2,000 to 10,000 men a side'; but he admits that 'the whole social fabric was affected by the general state of misrule' until the strong Tudor monarchy came into power.

The larger houses, in 1350, were still fortified. Stokesay Castle, built in *c.* 1240–90 (Fig. 30), is a typical and well-preserved example, but the charming half-timbered gatehouse shown in my sketch was added much later, *c.* 1570. Penshurst Place in Kent (1388) is a castellated and moated stronghold, but its fine Great Hall (Fig. 31) does show an advance in comfort, dignity, and beauty on the halls of the Norman feudal castles. My sketch is taken from the 'high table', on a 'dais' where the owner sat with his guests, looking down the hall where the 'screens', with the minstrels' gallery above them, shielded the doors leading to the kitchen, pantry, larders, and buttery. On either side of the hall were long tables to accommodate the retainers, and there was a central hearth on which a log-fire blazed, the smoke rising to the open roof and escaping through a louvred ventilator at the ridge. This is the type of hall which may be seen in the old colleges of Oxford and Cambridge. Glass painted with heraldic emblems filled the fine traceried windows. Behind the 'high table', a door led into the 'solar' (private sitting-room for the family) or 'withdrawing-room': hence our modern word 'drawing-room'. Carpets were now introduced, and walls came to be hung with tapestry ('Arras cloth') or panelled in oak. Other examples of the period 1350–1400 are Bodiam Castle in Sussex, Haddon Hall in Derbyshire, and Kenilworth Castle in Warwickshire.

In the fifteenth century, the general introduction of gunpowder made these fortified houses less impregnable, but many of the larger dwellings retained a measure of protection against marauding bands. Examples are Tattershall Castle in Lincolnshire, the keep of Warkworth Castle in Northumberland, Kirby Muxloe Castle in Leicestershire, South Wingfield Manor-house in Derbyshire, and Oxburgh Hall in Norfolk. Far more domestic in character are the manor-houses of Great Chalfield in Wiltshire and Cothay in Somerset; while at Lower Brockhampton Manor-house in Herefordshire and at the lovely 'Paycockes' house at Coggeshall in Essex we find the elaborate half-timber construction which reached a high level during the sixteenth and early seventeenth centuries (pp. 132, 135). The magnificent stone-built kitchens at Glastonbury and at Stanton Harcourt in Oxfordshire (both fifteenth century) must be mentioned here.

The position of the 'lower orders' of society was still deplorable. Their huts continued to be built of timber and thatch and clay, and probably the type of cottage illustrated on Figs. 1, A and 1, B in this book was only available for the more fortunate peasants and artisans. Chimneys, glazed windows, and any form of sanitation were denied to them; where chimneys are found on cottages of this date they are usually later additions. The animals slept with the cottagers, even in London up to 1419!

Apart from dwelling-houses, this period saw the erection of two of our most famous school buildings—Winchester College (1382) and Eton College (1422); and of several of the oldest colleges at Oxford and Cambridge, all in the same late Gothic style already described in connexion with churches.

This chapter may well conclude with a brief description of the way in which building was carried out during the late Gothic period in England. Ample evidence is now available from authentic historical records. As the reader will have inferred, the two great forces in building were the Church and the Crown. The former category includes the monasteries, the 'secular' cathedrals, and the parish-churches, large and small. The person who authorized and commissioned an important church was invariably a cleric of some sort, and the documents, generally in Latin, record '*fieri fecit*', i.e. that 'he caused it to be made'. That is quite different from stating that 'he designed it'. Thus William of Wykeham, a most able and pushful ecclesiastic, did cause a great deal of important building to be carried out, including his own foundations of Winchester College and of New College at Oxford; and a man of his 'drive' and power would certainly have a good deal to say as to the precise requirements in accommodation. It would be surprising, too, if he did not express his opinions on the style and appearance of the building. But, granting all these probabilities, it is no more likely that he designed it himself than that Mr. Gordon Selfridge designed his own huge store when 'he caused it to be made' in Oxford Street a generation ago.

No; William of Wykeham, who figured in the list of famous English architects in early Victorian books, has long been transferred from that position to the honourable status of a 'noble patron'. The great ecclesiastics, whether monastic or 'secular', employed architects to carry out their buildings, in England as on the Continent, and the names of most of them are known in the case of the largest churches. The same applies to the royal castles, palaces, and other buildings, which were erected under the direction of a Government department corresponding exactly to our modern Ministry of Works and Public Buildings. In the fourteenth century, one Geoffrey Chaucer (1340–1400), after a most varied career as a page at Court, a soldier, and a holder of divers posts in the Civil Service of the day, served for a short time as a 'clerk-of-works' on royal buildings, but nobody has ever suggested that he acted as architect.

In describing the actual designer and supervisor of buildings in the Middle Ages, the term 'architect' was seldom used in any European country until Latin ideas were reintroduced during the sixteenth century; but that fact does not prove that no such functionary was employed: only that we must look for him under another name. It is a simple common-sense deduction that some person with technical ability must have conceived and executed any building of an elaborate nature: no king or abbot or bishop or committee could have done it. In fact, the medieval architect in England usually appears as 'Master' (*Magister* in Latin), not as 'master-mason' or 'master-carpenter', though such personages worked with him. The architect, in supreme charge of the undertaking, had usually risen from the ranks of the master-masons, because the most important part of a medieval building was the masonry.

Other established facts about medieval architects are that they were not invariably confined to the design and supervision of one commission at a time but that they sometimes carried on a 'practice', that they travelled about to see other buildings and glean fresh ideas for improving their own, that they sketched such buildings, and that they used plans on parchment. Very few of such drawings have been preserved, because parchment was very precious: after it had been used once for plans and had served its purpose, the ink was erased, and then the parchment was used again and again until it finally came to pieces. The finest architectural drawings of the late Gothic period are those preserved at Cologne Cathedral. Other personages connected with large building enterprises were described as 'Supervisor', 'Surveyor', 'Master of the Works' and 'Devizor'—all concerned with finance, provision of materials and labour, payment of wages, &c. Several medieval specifications and many complete accounts for large building works have been discovered.

As for the general body of craftsmen and labourers, it is essential to remember that these men were human beings, of like passions with ourselves; and that the Middle Ages cannot be regarded indiscriminately as 'the good old times'. It is no more conceivable that all this motley crowd of artisans worked assiduously and harmoniously for the glory of God than that our splendid cathedrals sprouted up from the ground without plans or the skilled direction of an architect. Historical documents record fines for idleness, brawling, unpunctuality, obstruction of other workmen, and loss of tools. Wycliffe wrote of certain masons that they

conspire together that no man of their craft shall take less a day than they fix, though he should by good conscience take much less—that none of them shall do good steady work which might interfere with other men of the craft, and that none of them shall do anything but cut stone, though he might profit his master twenty pounds by one day's work by laying a wall, without harm to himself.

The various guilds of building crafts became immensely powerful and have survived in part to-day in the livery-companies of the City of London (e.g. Carpenters, Plumbers, Painter-Stainers, Plaisterers, Tylers, and Bricklayers), who continue to support technical training; also, many of their customs, ceremonies, and honorific titles have been adopted in freemasonry. Compared with modern craftsmen, it is certain that they were allowed more initiative in the matter of carved details, &c., and that apprenticeship was much more general than it is to-day. Hours of work were very long, usually from sunrise to sunset with twenty minutes interval for breakfast, sixty minutes in winter and ninety minutes in summer for dinner, and a few minutes for a drink in the afternoon. No work was done on the numerous saints' days ('holy-days'), and no pay was allowed for those days.

Transport of material was a serious problem at a time when there were no made roads or canals, so that everything had to be carried on pack-animals or floated down rivers. Water-transport was employed whenever possible, and it was often as easy to bring the fine Caen stone from Normandy across the Channel as to convey English stone overland from a distant quarry. Where pack-transport was the only means available and no quarry was at hand, a solution was often found in the use of small blocks of stone and a consequent change in methods of design. The records of many fine Gothic buildings in districts remote from quarries (e.g. East Anglia, London, Windsor, Kent) show what difficulties were encountered and surmounted in that respect.

With bad housing, prevalent disease, meagre wages, long hours, and an absence of most of the amenities of modern life, the medieval craftsman need not arouse our envy; but, even if all the absurd legends of his saintly and selfless labour be discounted, the sum of his achievement remains a standing marvel and an inspiration to us all.

CHAPTER 9

THE DAWN OF THE RENAISSANCE IN ENGLISH ARCHITECTURE (*c.* 1550–1620)

FOR A century or more, the French word 'Renaissance' has been used in England to describe a great movement, and also to define a period or style of architecture resulting from that movement. Foreign words always embarrass us, and so many people boggle at pronouncing 'Renaissance', hesitating whether or not to give it a Parisian lilt, that there is something to be said for substituting 'Renascence', as many scholars now do. So far as English architecture is concerned, the Renaissance really dawned in the first half of the sixteenth century, began to influence design about 1550, attained maturity under Inigo Jones about 1620, continued to develop under Wren and his followers until late Georgian times, and finally petered out in the days of the Regency; thus covering a span of nearly three centuries, to which three chapters of this book are devoted. 'Renaissance' means, of course, 'rebirth'; but in architecture it means more precisely the rebirth of Roman architecture, after four centuries of Gothic. Yet it may be argued that the influence of Rome in our architecture had never wholly lapsed, that there is a continuity from the ancient basilicas in Rome itself to the basilican churches in Kent and at Brixworth (pp. 60-1), from them to our 'Romanesque' round-arched churches—first Saxon and then Norman—and so all the way to our late Gothic examples. That is true; on the other hand, the process had been gradual, and the sudden leap backwards from late Gothic to the Roman fashions of more than a thousand years earlier was a very different matter.

The Renaissance in architecture reached us from Italy very late, and its influence had made itself felt in other aspects of cultural life long before that. In the realm of literature the 'New Learning', as John Richard Green calls it, is considered to have had its birth in the time of the Italian poet Petrarch (1304–74), who revived an interest in classical scholarship and brought new ideas of cheerful, joyous humanism into a world controlled by clerical dogmatists. The heyday of the Italian Renaissance is usually located at the court of the Medici family in Florence from *c.* 1450 to 1490; and by 1550, when the 'New Learning' was rapidly spreading through England, the pendulum was swinging back in Italy as the Jesuits introduced their 'Counter Reformation' and re-established clerical domination.

In England, its arrival coincided with the Dissolution of the Monasteries in 1536–9 and the establishment in 1531 of the Protestant Church of England, detached from the Papacy. It is significant that this chapter is concerned exclusively with secular buildings; for, not only were no new monasteries built, but not a single church of any importance was erected in England during the period 1550–1620, though great numbers of large Catholic churches were built in Continental Europe during those seventy years. There is a tiny Congregational chapel at Horningsham in Wiltshire which is dated 1566, built for Scottish masons employed at lordly Longleat hard by. This fact reminds us that organized Nonconformity was born in Elizabeth's reign (among advanced Protestants who held that the Reformation did not go far enough) and that it was generally suppressed. Much of the image-breaking usually attributed to Oliver Cromwell was in fact carried out a century before his day, by his namesake Thomas Cromwell, a pillar of the new Protestant Church of England.

Instead of churches, many schools and colleges were founded; and a great boom in house-building began. Thus the effects of the Reformation and the Renaissance, occurring simultaneously, were tremendous in our social life. The long rule of the Pope was over; the monks, nuns, and friars—numbering perhaps 8,600 in all— were pensioned off; and their magnificent estates and buildings were sold by Henry VIII in order to bolster up his personal and national funds. The purchasers, noblemen or wealthy merchants, either occupied and modernized the monastic buildings or demolished them to obtain materials for splendid mansions and manor-houses.

The Elizabethan system [writes Professor Trevelyan] was as much a triumph of the Renaissance as of the Reformation. The two became one, and partly for that reason Shakespeare's England had a charm and lightness of heart, a free aspiring of mind and spirit not to be found in the harsh Jesuit-Calvinist Europe of that day.

At Henry VIII's court,

the gentlemen of England learned not only the intrigues of love and politics, but music and poetry, and a taste for scholarship and the arts, seeds which they took back to their rural homes to plant there. . . . Peace and order at last prevailed in the land. . . . The old Hebrew and the Graeco-Roman ways of life, raised from the grave of the remote past by the magic of scholarship, were opened to the general understanding of Englishmen, who treated them not as dead archaeological matter, but as new spheres of imagination and spiritual power, to be freely converted to modern use.

Let us consider how the seeds of Renaissance architecture found their way to England. The first apostle of the new way of building was Filippo Brunelleschi of Florence (1377–1446), who went as a young man, with his friend Donatello, to Rome in or about 1402 to make a study of the neglected ruins of the Imperial temples and palaces. His object was, in part at any rate, to devise some method of raising a dome over the unfinished cathedral in his native city, then a subject of public competition among architects, and in fact he realized his ambition, for his dome was a success; but he also acquired an intense admiration for the architecture of ancient Rome, and started a fashion for reviving it which other architects soon followed. At about the same time, in 1414, the manuscript of Vitruvius' famous book on architecture (p. 1) was discovered in a Swiss monastery, and in 1486 it was published in print. The effect was amazing: it ran through edition after edition, in many languages; then other books of 'The Orders' followed, based upon Vitruvius, including one by Andrea Palladio in 1570 which also became a 'best-seller' and had an enormous influence on English architecture, as explained in Chapter 10. Soon the educated classes in England were infected with this antiquarian enthusiasm, and in 1550 the Duke of Northumberland sent an English architect named John Shute to Italy to report first-hand and bring back some 'souvenirs': one result was Shute's book, *The Chief Groundes of Architecture*, published in 1563.

As we shall see, these books played a considerable part in spreading the glad tidings of 'The Orders' through England, and indeed some critics have stigmatized the new style as 'the architecture of a book' (i.e. Vitruvius' book); but the earliest heralds of the dawn were individual Italian craftsmen, commissioned by wealthy patrons of the arts to furnish architectural bric-à-brac

32. HENRY THE SEVENTH'S TOMB,
WESTMINSTER ABBEY

in the fashionable new mode from overseas. Probably the first among them was Pietro Torrigiano, an architectural sculptor, who contracted with Henry VIII in 1511 to make the tomb of Lady Margaret Beaufort and in 1512 to make another tomb for the King's parents, Henry VII and Elizabeth of York, both in Westminster Abbey. The latter tomb, illustrated in Fig. 32, is a splendid work of purely Italian art, with nothing Gothic or English about it, though Gothic churches were still being built by English masons at that time. It consists of a black marble sarcophagus, divided by pilasters of gilded bronze into panels containing bronze bas-reliefs, and with delightfully pagan gilt-bronze cherubs perched precariously on the four corners. The two magnificent effigies reclining on the sarcophagus are also of gilded bronze. Shortly afterwards, Torrigiano, with three assistants obtained from Italy, executed the high altar (since destroyed) for Henry VII's Chapel.

Another interesting piece of work by an Italian craftsman is the series of terracotta medallions and busts of Roman emperors at Hampton Court Palace, commissioned by Cardinal Wolsey c. 1520 from Giovanni da Majano. These busts were built into the walls of a new but completely Gothic and English building. Ornamental plasterwork by Italians was a feature of the celebrated Nonsuch Palace near Cheam in Surrey, unfortunately demolished in 1670. The list might be extended, but the point to bear in mind is that all the work done by Italians up to the time of Henry's death in 1547—after which we hear no more of them —consists of relatively small ornamental details, and includes no buildings. This work was all commissioned by the King and his chief courtiers.

The next wave of alien influence came from Germany, France, and the Low Countries, transmitted mainly by refugees from Catholic persecution during the wars of 'religion'. Some of the German and Flemish copybooks of the Orders (e.g. that by Vredeman de Vries, published in 1563) are crude caricatures of graceful Greek and Roman forms; and the undoubted ostentation and vulgarity of such great houses as Wollaton Hall near

Nottingham (1580–8) is due to the corrupt sources from which classical inspiration was derived. Yet much charming craftsmanship may be attributed to these refugees, e.g. carved Jacobean pulpits in many country churches (made obligatory in every parish-church in 1603), and quaint brick gables in East Anglia, recalling the streets of Bruges or Haarlem.

Instructed to some extent in person by visitors from overseas, taught in equal or larger measure by various foreign books of 'The Orders', our English builders had begun to introduce Renaissance ideas and elements into their designs, especially for the mansions of the new nobility and the followers of the Court, by the middle of the century. Sometimes the adventures were almost ludicrous, as in the case of the 'Tower of the Five Orders', clumsily applied to the Gothic front of the Bodleian Library at Oxford: both the Renaissance and the Gothic portions were built simultaneously in 1613–19.

Much more important than these experiments in pastiche is the slow but sweeping change that gradually transformed the stark fortified dwelling of the fifteenth century into the gracious and spacious Elizabethan house. Examples of the former type (p. 116) were usually approached by a drawbridge across a moat, and entered through a gateway with or without a portcullis. They were grouped round one or more courtyards. Whatever may have been their actual defensive value, they were planned with the apparent purpose of defence. Battlements still crowned the lofty outer walls. Each house contained one fine apartment, the 'Great Hall' already described, and often a private chapel, but the remaining rooms seldom possessed any dignity. In Elizabeth's day, young men of fashion began to visit Italy, and returned with ideas of cultured living and domestic comfort which accorded ill with the somewhat crude conditions prevailing in their own households. Most of the large houses built about 1550 retained the quadrangular plan, with the central gate-tower and battlements, but the Great Hall was usually placed centrally on the inner side of the quadrangle, facing the entrance; and this plan was adopted in most of the Elizabethan colleges at Oxford and Cambridge. As Elizabethan ideas of 'sweetness and light' began to spread, the entrance-block of the quadrangle came to be omitted—indeed it was actually demolished in some instances, e.g. Sutton Place near Guildford and Athelhampton Hall in Dorset. Life was now becoming more civilized, and the need for spacious and beautiful rooms was felt, eventually leading to that crowning glory of Elizabethan and Jacobean architecture, the 'Long Gallery'. This magnificent apartment was generally placed on the first floor, and ran from end to end of the house. It usually overlooked the gardens which now formed an integral feature of the design.

Aston Hall near Birmingham (Fig. 33), built in 1618–35 at the very end of the Jacobean period, stands in an industrial district defaced by squalor and smoke, but is illustrated here as a typical example of English domestic architecture just before the full tide of the Italian Renaissance swept away our Gothic tradition. My sketch shows the entrance front; usually at the back is a garden front with a terrace. Here the splendid forecourt is open in front, and the whole lay-out is absolutely symmetrical, a contrast to the picturesque irregularity of late Gothic houses. Little garden-pavilions at the outer angles of the forecourt emphasize

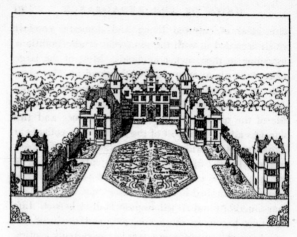

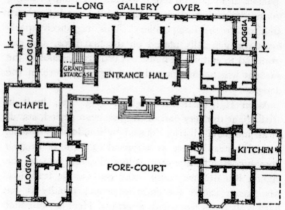

33. ASTON HALL, BIRMINGHAM, c. 1620

(*above*) Air view (the formal gardens have been recently restored by the Birmingham Civic Society

(*below*) Ground Plan

the formality of the scheme, and the space between them and the mansion is filled with a *parterre* of flower-beds bordered with box edging, entirely in the Italian manner. This formal approach was well suited to the stilted manners of the Elizabethan age, when the Queen, arriving in the course of a 'royal progress' to quarter herself with a numerous retinue on a possibly unwilling host, would be met by a bevy of Greek shepherds or Roman nymphs, who would spout poetry to her in their dead languages. Mingled with all this formality in some of the gardens were such 'quaint conceits' from Italy as a grotto with hidden taps that suddenly drenched the guests with water as they stepped upon a concealed spring in the pavement. Less embarrassing to the visitors were the water-organs that warbled German hymn-tunes or Neapolitan operatic airs without any visible provocation.

The stately pageantry in these great formal gardens, which fell away in successive terraces towards the surrounding views, was matched within the house, especially in the Long Gallery, which, at Aston Hall, measures 136 feet long, 18 feet wide, and 16 feet high. The walls are panelled in oak from end to end, in rather small panels of a curious design. The length of the wall is divided up by tall flat pilasters (flat columns) of a modified Roman type, extending from floor to ceiling. Each small panel contains a flat semicircular arch, also resting on Roman pilasters. So here, in the decoration of this thoroughly English room, we find our old friend the Roman 'Order' appearing, after many centuries of hibernation overseas. The ornamental plasterwork of Tudor and Elizabethan ceilings was mainly designed and executed by Italians after its first introduction in the

sixteenth century, and contained many Italian details
of design, but some of the Elizabethan examples are
very English in character. Besides fine panelling and
plasterwork, the Long Gallery always contained a range
of noble mullioned windows, and one or more great
stone fireplaces loaded with heraldry and carved symbolism. The larger Elizabethan houses also generally
possessed a dignified oak staircase, with massive carved
newel-posts, heavy ornamental balusters and handrails,
and perhaps a pair of 'dog-gates' at the bottom, to
prevent the hounds straying into the bedrooms. The
Hall, at the beginning of Elizabethan times, remained
the sole dining-room and sitting-room, as in medieval
days, but by 1620 it had generally become a mere central
vestibule, though at Aston it is an imposing room, 47
by 24 feet. Family sitting-rooms were now provided in
all these large houses. Externally, the Elizabethan and
Jacobean mansions exhibit an advance upon Tudor
buildings in their greater symmetry and stateliness.
From Italy are introduced strong horizontal lines in
cornices and parapets, with columns and pilasters and
entablatures everywhere. But the English fashion of
mullioned windows, bold gables, turrets, and pinnacles
persists.

The design of these great houses, which are scattered
all over our country, varies according to the materials
available locally. Thus we find rather rough masonry
in the Yorkshire dales, Westmorland and Derbyshire;
finer and more delicate masonry in the limestone
district, including the Cotswolds, that extends right
across England from Dorset to Lincolnshire; timber
framing or 'half-timber work' in the West Midlands,
Cheshire, and Kent; brick in East Anglia and the

34. A YORKSHIRE STONE HOUSE:
GUISELEY RECTORY

35. COTSWOLD STONE COTTAGES
AT BIBURY, GLOUCESTERSHIRE

remaining counties. Among a host of examples, the following may be cited as particularly important. In north-country stone: Wollaton Hall near Nottingham (p. 126); Haddon Hall, Bolsover Castle, and Hardwick Hall in Derbyshire; Sizergh Castle in Westmorland; Fountains Hall in Yorkshire. In limestone: Athelhampton Hall in Dorset; Kirby Hall and Burghley House in Northamptonshire; Montacute, Longleat, and Barrington Court in Somerset; Chastleton House in Oxfordshire; Audley End in Essex; Knole in Kent. In half-timber: Moreton Old Hall and Bramhall House in Cheshire; Speke Hall in Lancashire. In brick with stone dressings: Hatfield House in Hertfordshire; Holland House at Kensington; Blickling Hall in Norfolk; Temple Newsam near Leeds; Bramshill House in Hampshire; and Aston Hall just described.

Apart from these 'lordly seats', the period 1550–1620 saw the building of a great number of charming manor-houses and cottages which, generally speaking, were far less influenced by Italian fashions and 'quaint conceits' in architecture. The Gothic tradition which had become so integral a part of our building crafts died very reluctantly, and thus we find mullioned windows, bold chimneys, and steep gabled roofs persisting long after Inigo Jones had succeeded in imposing the austere doctrines of Palladio upon Court circles in London— indeed one can find rustic Gothic features in remote districts right up to 1700 or even later. Figs. 34 and 35 provide a comparison between Yorkshire stone houses and those of the 'Cotswold' limestone belt. Fig. 34 illustrates the Rectory at Guiseley in Yorkshire, with a low-pitched roof covered with heavy stone 'slates', well suited to resist the rather grim weather of the Yorkshire dales; while Fig. 35 represents a lovely group of cottages at Bibury in Gloucestershire, more dainty in character, with steeper roofs and smaller stone 'slates'. Similarly Figs. 36 and 37 present a contrast in half-timber work. The 'Old House' at Hereford, though erected as late as 1621, is Gothic in every line, and thoroughly picturesque; and the wing of Little Moreton Hall or Moreton Old Hall (1559), illustrated in Fig. 37, is one of the most startling examples of ambitious rustic carpentry in all England. My sketch does not show the marvellous polygonal bay-windows of the inner courtyard, which bear this remarkable but quite excusable inscription: 'Richard Dale, Carpenter, made these windows by the grace of God.' In Kent, half-timbered houses are far more reticent in design, the framework consisting of closely-spaced uprights and massive horizontal beams, with few of the ornamental braces found in the West Midlands; but all these old houses are honestly constructed of heavy solid timbers fastened together with oak pins at their framed joints. It is sad that this characteristic English mode of construction has been so unmercifully caricatured by modern speculative builders, who have substituted for the massive posts and beams of our forefathers a system of flimsy boards merely tacked on to a brick background.

In East Anglia, where stone is scarce, the smaller houses were constructed of timber framing, but the exterior was usually 'parged' with a thick coat of tough, leathery plaster, composed of lime mixed with hair, protecting the timber framing beneath. In recent years, many of these houses have been stripped of their facing in order to expose the oak timbers, often to their detriment. In Essex, Hertfordshire, Middlesex, and

36. THE 'OLD HOUSE', HEREFORD

37. MORETON OLD HALL, CHESHIRE

some parts of Kent, framed houses were covered with weather-boarding (Fig. 38), which likewise afforded excellent protection. This mode of building was carried over to America in 1620 by the 'Pilgrim Fathers', of whom the greater number came from these south-eastern counties, and was adopted for their earliest houses (Fig. 56) and churches in 'New England'. It cannot be pretended that Chequers Court (Fig. 39), built in 1565, is a small house; indeed it has provided a home for our harassed Prime Ministers since Lord Lee gave it to the nation in 1917, but it is an excellent example of the less ostentatious domestic architecture of its period. Lastly may be mentioned the attractive habit of covering the fronts of timber-framed houses with tile-hanging, prevalent especially in Surrey and the adjoining counties; but this method is picturesque rather than ancient. Many competent foreign writers regard our minor domestic buildings of the sixteenth and seventeenth centuries as our best architecture: certainly they afford a profitable field for study.

At Oxford and Cambridge, as might be expected, the Renaissance in architecture, as in letters, was welcomed with open arms; and, as one famous historian has caustically observed, 'the studies and learning of the Middle Ages crumbled like a corpse exposed to the air'. Some of the experiments in the new style were, however, very crude, including the 'Tower of the Five Orders' at Oxford, already mentioned; and the popularly admired 'Gate of Honour' at Caius College, Cambridge (1575), has always struck me as a travesty of Italian design. On the other hand, much of the best architecture in both universities dates from this period, and often shows very little Italian influence, e.g. the front of Wadham College

K

38. WEATHERBOARDED HOUSES AT GREAT WAKERING, ESSEX

39. CHEQUERS COURT, BUCKINGHAMSHIRE

at Oxford (1610–13). Many of our older grammar-schools date from the second half of the sixteenth century and some of them still possess their original buildings. Other secular monuments of note erected during the reigns of Elizabeth and James I include the halls of Gray's Inn and the Middle Temple, the splendid half-timber front of Staple Inn, the hall of the Charterhouse —all in London; the Whitgift Hospital at Croydon; and Abbot's Hospital at Guildford.

It was in the reign of Elizabeth that the title of 'architect' first came into general use, but there is some uncertainty as to his exact status and function. The epitaph of Robert Smithson (d. 1614) describes him as 'gent, architector and survayor unto the most worthy house of Wollaton with others of great account'; but, unfortunately, Wollaton Hall is one of the most vulgar designs of the day. Another somewhat dim figure is John Thorpe, who has been credited with many of the great mansions of the period, including Aston Hall where I discovered his initials. Both he and the Smithson family have left most interesting collections of drawings, but there is no conclusive evidence that all the buildings illustrated on those drawings were in fact designed by them. A third name is that of Ralph Simons, who is believed to have designed much collegiate work at Cambridge between 1584 and 1605. In the next chapter the architect comes into his own.

CHAPTER 10

INIGO JONES AND CHRISTOPHER WREN
(1620–1714)

ALTHOUGH THE architectural history of this important period is dominated by the familiar names that head this chapter, it is so closely interwoven with, and influenced by, social history that even the changes in architectural form may be attributed to religious and social factors. During the first seventy of these ninety-four years, England was in a state of political turmoil, most unfavourable to building progress, and much of the unrest was due to religious causes. It began in Elizabeth's reign, when the repression of the Roman Catholics and the persecution of the Protestant Dissenters, or 'Separatists' as they were then called, was severe. It went on abreast of Elizabeth's royal progresses and classical pageants, all through the golden age of Shakespeare; and religious intolerance continued throughout the first two Stuart reigns, resulting in the emigration of the 'Pilgrim Fathers' to 'New England' in 1620 (pp. 202–4). In the later years of Charles I, who had married a Roman Catholic princess, things came to a head; and, as every reader of this book will know, the Civil War of 1642–6 was a struggle to the death between the Royalists, the aristocracy and the conservative party within the Church on the one hand, and the forces of Parliament, Puritanism, and the London citizens on the other. Hardly any churches were erected between 1620 and 1660, and it is easy to see why church-building was so negligible in the earlier half of the seventeenth century.

Under the Commonwealth, the Puritans took their revenge on the Church of England for the persecution they had endured in the preceding era. Many of the 'popish' trappings that the zealous Churchman Thomas Cromwell had stripped from the churches a century before had since been reinstated; and now a second campaign ensued, often senseless and brutal, but always inspired, it must be remembered, by fierce resentment for the cruelties suffered by the Puritans in times past. Many clergymen were ejected from their livings, often with good cause, and Nonconformist services were held in some of the cathedrals.

In 1660 the pendulum swung back again, violently; and two years later came the most sweeping purge of all, when 2,000 clergymen, including many of the most famous divines in London and the universities, were turned out and replaced by priests of Royalist sympathies. Thus, when the Great Fire of London in 1666 destroyed a large number of Gothic churches in the City, no serious objection was raised to their being rebuilt out of public funds, and thus Wren had his first great chance as an architect (p. 150). Meanwhile, French and Jesuit influences from abroad, which had smouldered under Charles II, blazed up after his death, and his successor was deposed in 1689. The arrival of William of Orange in that year had two obvious effects upon our architecture: it led to the introduction of many Dutch features into English design; and, by the passing of the Toleration Act, Dissenters were permitted to build their own 'chapels' or 'meeting-houses'. Even the architecture of Anglican churches assumed a more definitely Protestant character under Wren, and the Roman Catholics suffered a complete eclipse. Everything that savoured of Jesuitry, including the 'Baroque' architecture then fashionable in Rome and the Catholic countries, was received with distrust in this country, though Baroque did have some influence upon Wren and his disciples. In Queen Anne's reign (1702–14), England settled down at last to a placid, prosperous, and comparatively tolerant existence which Wren lived to see, for his death did not occur till 1723.

Retracing our steps now to the amazing career of Inigo Jones (1573–1652), another long-lived man, we find that little is known of his early days except that he was born in Smithfield, London, and that his father, a clothworker, was fined for using bad language to a lady. Inigo cannot have had any extensive education, and it seems probable that his youth was spent in the study of drawing rather than at a joiner's bench, as Horace Walpole suggested. There is evidence, however, that in 1601 he was studying in Italy, and it seems likely that he spent a considerable time thus, though it is difficult to disentangle his first from his second visit, which definitely took place in 1612–14. It was, apparently, as a result of these studies that he was engaged by King Christian IV of Denmark to carry out some unknown architectural work. As that monarch was brother to Anne of Denmark, James I's queen, it may reasonably be inferred that Inigo's introduction to the English court was directly due to his Danish commission; and in 1605 he was employed by the University of Oxford to stage three plays for a visit by the king. He was described on that occasion as 'a great traveller, who undertook to further them much, and furnish them with rare Devices'. He was thus

employed as an expert in theatrical *décor*, but primarily
in order to provide the authentic Italian note which was
then so fashionable, for architects of the type mentioned
on p. 139 had acquired only a smattering of classical
prototypes from garbled versions in the copybooks,
whereas he had studied the monuments at first-hand.
As he himself wrote at a later date:

Being naturally inclined in my younger years to study
the arts of design, I passed into foreign parts to converse
with the great masters thereof in Italy; where I applied
myself to search out the ruins of those ancient buildings
which, in spite of Time itself, and violence of barbarians,
are yet remaining.

In fact, he was Brunelleschi over again!

The performance of plays and masques before the
Court had begun in Elizabeth's reign, and continued
to be very popular under her two successors. Inigo
Jones seems to have mastered the mechanism of stage-
furniture as well as its design, and was the inventor of
movable scenery. Sacheverell Sitwell describes him as
'the first and greatest English artist of the theatre'. In
1614, however, he was appointed Surveyor-General to
the King, and soon began to produce the architectural
masterpieces which have made his chief reputation. The
buildings which can be reliably ascribed to him are
very few, though many others have been groundlessly
attributed to him in the past; but the two to be described
here are undoubtedly his work and are of great importance in the history of English architecture.

The old Banqueting House in the Tudor Palace of
Whitehall was burnt down on 12 January 1619. Less
than six months later, it is recorded that the new

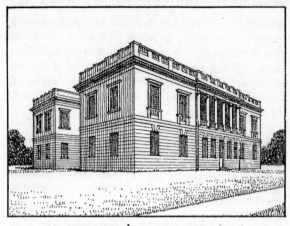

40. THE QUEEN'S HOUSE, GREENWICH:
AS ORIGINALLY BUILT

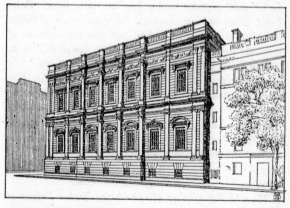

41. THE BANQUETING HOUSE, WHITEHALL, LONDON

Banqueting House (Fig. 41) had been begun, and in March 1622 it was completed: quick work if those dates are reliable. There is nothing English about the design, and the sudden change of fashion may be realized by comparing it with Aston Hall (Fig. 33), built at the same time; or with any typically Jacobean house. On the other hand, it would have been perfectly at home in any street of the Italian town of Vicenza, where Palladio built many palaces during the third quarter of the sixteenth century, i.e. about a generation before Inigo could have seen them.

Andrea Palladio (1518–80) was a very studious person who had made measured drawings of many Roman ruins and published a book of them with elaborate rules for their proportions, more meticulous than anything in the work of Vitruvius and his later commentators. Inigo used Palladio's book as his bible, and, though Wren treated architecture in a much more free and unacademic way, the worship of Palladio's rules was again revived in the eighteenth century (p. 157), and they dictated English architectural design over a period of many years. Instead of the picturesque gables and bold chimneys, the Gothic mullioned windows, and the heraldic devices of Jacobean buildings such as Aston Hall or Wadham College, we find, in this exotic building in Whitehall, a low roof hidden by a balustrade, large windows set at regular intervals (originally with solid frames though now fitted with sliding sashes), and all the formal panoply of the Orders. Set down suddenly in front of this austere but majestic façade, a Roman of 2,000 years ago would experience no feeling of surprise. Internally there is one magnificent room upstairs, 108 by 52 feet, with a flat ceiling divided into painted panels, as utterly unlike the Tudor Hall of Hampton Court Palace as this exterior is unlike any Tudor building.

Up to a few years ago, it was erroneously believed that the Banqueting House was a mere fraction or instalment of a huge palace covering an area 1,280 by 950 feet, with a frontage to St. James's Park on the west and to the river on the east. There was an enormous central courtyard 800 by 400 feet, and six lesser courts, one of which was circular. The plans were found among a collection of drawings belonging to John Webb (1611–72), Inigo's pupil; and J. A. Gotch has proved that Webb was the author of this splendid design, into which he had very skilfully dovetailed the Banqueting House, *already built*. Webb has now come to be recognized as an architect equal in ability to Jones and Wren, and to have been responsible for many buildings hitherto attributed to Inigo, including the so-called 'King Charles's Block' at Greenwich Palace, for which he was appointed architect in 1666.

However, there is no doubt that Inigo Jones designed the Queen's House at Greenwich, built between 1617 and 1635 (Fig. 40). To my mind, this is an infinitely more beautiful building than the Banqueting House, and shows the character of mature Renaissance architecture at its best. It is similar in style to the famous palaces at Genoa and Milan erected in the later years of the sixteenth and early part of the seventeenth centuries. and has an affinity to the fine château of Maisons near Paris, built in 1642–51. The royal palace at Greenwich, now a naval hospital, consisted in 1617 of a rambling group of picturesque buildings in red brick. The summer villa erected by Inigo for the Queen straddled the public highway between the palace and the royal park; so that

Her Majesty could gain access direct into the park. The new house was most ingeniously planned with this requisite in view, and my sketch shows it *as originally designed*. Since 1617, the recesses through which the road passed have been filled up, colonnades have been added to connect the house with the other blocks of the hospital, and Inigo Jones's mullioned windows have been replaced by sash-windows slightly longer than the originals. On the other side of the house, and therefore not visible in my sketch, is a fine horse-shoe flight of steps leading up to the terrace and the ground floor. Internally there is an imposing but austere 'Great Hall' on the ground floor, with a gallery; some charming rooms upstairs; and the graceful loggia shown on my sketch, with Ionic columns. Nothing like this had ever before been seen in England, and it should be studied by all those who wish to know what the Renaissance of Roman architecture really implied.

Inigo Jones also built St. Paul's Church in Covent Garden, about 1631, but practically nothing of the original work remains, and we cannot be sure that the present structure faithfully reproduces his original scheme. It is a very severe classical design with Doric columns. As previously stated, very few churches were built between 1550 and 1660: a rare exception is the fine old church of St. John in Leeds, erected in 1634 in late Gothic style but with splendid Jacobean woodwork. St. Mary's at Warwick was rebuilt in 1694 after a fire, in a most extraordinary version of belated Gothic, mingled with Roman balusters and other incongruous features. At the secluded hamlet of Walpole near Halesworth in Suffolk there is a very early example of Puritan architecture in the little Congregational chapel, built *c.* 1647 in a most unecclesiastical style and still retaining its quaint pulpit. The spate of Nonconformist building that followed the Toleration Act of 1689 may be considered more conveniently after we have ascertained what Wren had to say about 'Protestant' churches and their design.

The name of Sir Christopher Wren, M.P. (1632–1723), is, quite rightly, almost a household word among English-speaking people. To most of them he is known as the greatest English architect in history, yet he was never trained as an architect and did not receive his first commission until he was forty years of age, and that through family influence. In the previous year, 1661, he had been appointed, without any technical qualification, as assistant to the Surveyor-General of Works; but that too seems to have been, as Sir Reginald Blomfield observes, 'a most discreditable job'. Nevertheless, it must be borne in mind that in 1661 Wren was already a very distinguished man, a founder-member of the Royal Society, a professor of astronomy, a renowned scientist, and the author of fifty-three inventions covering almost everything under the sun. He was a Fellow of All Souls and had written a treatise on trigonometry when he was fifteen. John Evelyn, one of the foremost intellects of the day, wrote of a visit to Oxford in 1654 that 'after dinner I visited that miracle of a youth Mr. Christopher Wren, nephew of the Bishop of Ely'; and again, two days later, described him as 'that prodigious young scholar'.

Wren was, therefore, a complete amateur when he stepped into architecture in his fortieth year, but a genius of such amazing versatility that he would have adorned any field of activity he could choose. Almost certainly he knew how to draw, while on the construc-tional side his inventive ability and his scientific knowledge stood him in good stead. Unlike Inigo Jones and most of his own disciples, he never visited Italy, and a lengthy sketching-tour in France in 1665 (possibly arranged to escape the plague) gave him his only direct insight into Continental architecture: that fact is of some significance. For whereas Inigo Jones at Greenwich and François Mansart at Maisons had closely followed the style practised by architects in northern Italy fifty years before them, Wren was influenced by French and Dutch fashions as well as by the Baroque architecture of the Roman architect Bernini (1598–1680), whom he met in Paris.

Wren's first building, the chapel of Pembroke College, Cambridge, is a scholarly and attractive design, with no hint of amateurishness about it. His next work, the Sheldonian Theatre at Oxford, is not particularly pleasing externally, but forms an excellent auditorium for ceremonies, and its roof is a triumph of scientific carpentry with a span of 70 feet and a flat ceiling. The design is frankly based upon the ancient Theatre of Marcellus at Rome, and the twelve stone terminal figures of forgotten worthies which decorate the boundary railing are consciously antique rather than impressive.

Just before the Fire of London broke out in 1666, Wren had been consulted about the repair of the old Gothic cathedral of St. Paul; and, a few days after the Fire, even before the ashes were cold, he presented the King with a masterly scheme for replanning the whole City. As is well known, that scheme was not adopted, mainly because 'vested interests' came into play and because the 'dispossessed persons', as we should now call them, agitated for a speedy return to their previous sites, domestic or commercial. Thus was lost a great opportunity, how great we realize only too vividly to-day; but Wren was commissioned to rebuild St. Paul's and the majority of the numerous City churches which had perished in the flames.

Before we pass to his work as an ecclesiastical architect, his other outstanding secular buildings may be mentioned. Chief among them is the truly magnificent block which he added to Hampton Court Palace for 'Dutch William' and his queen in 1689-1702. He made no attempt to harmonize this building, in height or design, with Wolsey's picturesque brick Tudor palace; but he did use brickwork, and brickwork of a quality which is a delight to the eye. He also used sash-windows, then a novelty, and he engaged the services of as talented a team of craftsmen in woodwork, plasterwork, masonry, wrought ironwork, and decorative painting as England has ever known. Compared with the colossal ostentation of the Younger Mansart's palace at Versailles, then just finished, Hampton Court is a modest effort; but from the point of view of sheer charm it is far superior, and is definitely English, in spite of Italian, French, and finally Dutch influence. Its beautiful formal gardens, too, set a new standard; and in that respect also it has a special attraction which is lacking in all the splendours of Versailles.

Besides much work at Oxford and Cambridge, including the curious quasi-Gothic 'Tom Tower' of Christ Church at the former and the library of Trinity College at the latter, Wren built a large part of the present Greenwich Hospital—a noble design with domes— Chelsea Hospital (which Carlyle aptly described as 'the work of a gentleman'), and Kensington Palace— including the famous Orangery, a perfect design.

42. GROOMBRIDGE PLACE, KENT

43. ST. PAUL'S CATHEDRAL, LONDON, IN 1942

Innumerable houses all over England have been ascribed to Wren, but doubt is now cast upon nearly all the attributions. Groombridge Place, Kent (Fig. 42), is one of them; and one may say of it that, even if Wren did not build it himself, it is exactly the sort of house he would have built. There are many somewhat similar houses in Holland, but these simple dwellings, found in all parts of our country, are essentially English. Though the sash-windows, the Doric columns of the porches, the hipped roofs, and the long horizontal lines of the eaves and cornice are all Renaissance features, nowhere in Italy will you find houses like these: they are part of our distinctive national heritage.

When all is said and done, however, Wren will go down to posterity as the brilliant designer of St. Paul's Cathedral and fifty-one City churches, of which every single one that the Victorians had not previously demolished was damaged more or less during the air-raids of 1940-5, two being completely destroyed. Wren made several designs for St. Paul's, one of them so incredibly hideous that it is best forgotten here; and the present building is a compromise. He wanted, above everything, a central dome which should dominate London as the huge Gothic spire of Old St Paul's had dominated it in the past; and, in order to combine a spacious auditorium with the maximum dramatic effect, he desired a 'Greek cross' plan, as in Byzantine churches, i.e. a plan in which nave, chancel, and transepts are all short and all of equal size. The clergy, on the other hand, demanded the traditional (Gothic) 'Latin cross' plan with a long nave for processions and a fairly long chancel to give the effect of mystery to the altar. In the end, Wren was driven to accept the Latin cross plan with the result we now see (Figs. 43, 44); but a huge and elaborate model of his Greek cross plan still exists in the cathedral. In spite of everything, he produced what is, in my opinion, the most beautiful dome in the world. In order to create the best effect externally, it had to be lofty and to be crowned with an imposing stone lantern; whereas internally, for effect, it had to be much lower, otherwise a cavernous space would have been created, as at Castle Howard (p. 160). So he built a great brick cone from the base of the dome to carry the tremendous weight of the lantern, and strengthened it with a massive iron chain. On this cone rests the heavy timber framing of the outer dome, which is covered with lead, and beneath it is the low hemispherical inner dome, plastered and painted (Fig. 44). The dome was an entirely new feature in English architecture, derived from Rome it is true, but influenced by the new domes which he had seen in Paris. The craftsmanship throughout St. Paul's is superb, and much of it is 'Baroque' in spirit, again derived from Italy, and especially from Rome of the Renaissance.

'Baroque' is a term of abuse or nickname—like 'Gothic' —used to describe the florid but bold and masculine form of architecture favoured by the Jesuits as part of their 'Counter Reformation' movement, and spread by them all over the Catholic countries of southern and central Europe. It never obtained a firm hold in Protestant England, but Wren utilized many of its features, especially in designing the steeples of many of the fifty-one new City churches. At a time when other buildings were, at most, three storeys high, they stood up bravely above the adjoining roofs and dominated all views of the City up to Victorian days. Not all these churches were furnished with steeples, but there were

L

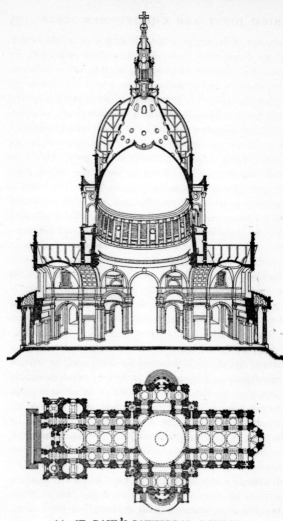

44. ST. PAUL'S CATHEDRAL, LONDON
(*above*) Section; (*below*) Plan

so many of them that variety of form was essential, and Wren found that variety in Baroque rather than in Palladian architecture. Internally, his concern was to provide an auditorium appropriate for Protestant (as opposed to Catholic) worship, with the pulpit, the organ, and the communion-table as essential features; and the planning of these structures, often on small and cramped sites, is universally agreed to be masterly, while the craftsmanship is as admirable as the design. In the later and larger churches which he built outside the City (e.g. St. James's, Piccadilly), he had to use galleries in order to contrive the necessary seating accommodation; and, in a long and most interesting memorandum which he wrote towards the end of his life, he gave his reasons, the fruits of lengthy experience, for his 'Protestant' planning, with the hope of helping other architects then building the fifty new London churches ordered by Queen Anne in 1711.

The various Nonconformist bodies—Congregationalists, Baptists, and Presbyterians—built their less ambitious meeting-houses on the same lines; but, as they were dependent on freewill offerings instead of on public funds, they were seldom wealthy enough to afford the rich decoration found in so many of Wren's churches. There are good examples in 'Old Meeting' at Norwich (1693), Friar Street Chapel at Ipswich (1700), and Churchgate Street Chapel at Bury St. Edmunds (1711). Even more unpretending are the modest Quaker meeting-houses of the period, of which the charming little specimen at Jordans in Buckinghamshire (1688) is the best known and the most attractive. No church buildings of this era, from St. Paul's Cathedral down to the lowliest meeting-house, were built in the Gothic style.

LATE RENAISSANCE ARCHITECTURE IN ENGLAND (1714–1820)

IN CHAPTER 7 it was explained how difficult it is to separate into watertight compartments the story of a progressive development in building. The same dilemma occurs in the long history of the English Renaissance between *c.* 1550 and *c.* 1820, but some subdivision is desirable for convenience of treatment, and it cannot be made satisfactorily by centuries. The scope of this chapter approximately covers 'Georgian' architecture, but stops short of the conflict between the 'Greek' and 'Gothic' Revivals, which began about 1820: and it nearly corresponds to the eighteenth century, but excludes the reign of Queen Anne, in which Wren was still practising.

The period now to be discussed begins just after the Battle of Blenheim in 1704 and ends just after the Battle of Waterloo, with the Seven Years War as a halfway house. Yet, in spite of these three considerable campaigns abroad, there was no civil war at home, and thus the times were favourable to building. England was relatively prosperous and certainly complacent. The Church of England was tolerant in comparison with the previous century, and the Dissenters continued to build their chapels. Gibbon's celebrated gibe at 'the fat slumbers of the Church' in his day, so often quoted, is perhaps unjustified; but the fact remains that very few churches were erected between 1714 and 1820; less than a dozen of the quota of fifty ordered by Queen Anne for London in 1711 were actually built, and consideration of these may be relegated to the end of this chapter, together with the first architecture of Methodism. The appalling sloth and obscurantism pervading the universities of Oxford and Cambridge, at that time 'close ecclesiastical corporations' ridden with pride and prejudice, has been vividly pictured by Professor Trevelyan: hence the comparative lack of notable additions to their buildings between c. 1740 and c. 1830, though a few designs of the earlier part of the century will shortly be mentioned.

Except for an occasional 'model village', laid out by some nobleman at his palatial gates (e.g. Harewood in Yorkshire), not much attention seems to have been given to the housing of the poorer classes, and in the latter part of the eighteenth century the 'Industrial Revolution' tempted people to migrate in crowds to the new smoky towns of the North and the Midlands, with the lamentable results that we all know. On the other hand, England is studded with innumerable small 'Georgian' houses for the middle class, conspicuous for refined detail. Some of these were doubtless designed by architects; but more were designed by country builders armed with excellent little manuals written by architects (e.g. by James Gibbs), books which prescribed the appropriate mouldings for every conceivable feature, in addition to explaining 'the Orders' in simple terms. Once more, building became traditional, but now the tradition was Roman instead of Gothic. The elegance which marked these unpretentious dwellings in remote villages and sleepy market-towns extended to almost every manufactured article: furniture, china, silverware, embroidery. Taste did not remain static: there were Palladian, Baroque, Rococo, Chinese, Pompeian, and Greek infusions during the century, and these affected design in all the crafts, even wallpapers and carpets, but such vagaries may be discussed in connexion with their architect-sponsors, for the eighteenth century produced a series of most remarkable architectural personalities, several of them 'characters'.

Having successively eliminated the Church, the universities, and the mass of the people, we now come to the outstanding factor in eighteenth-century English architecture. It was essentially and overwhelmingly an aristocratic age. Horace Walpole, a 'man of taste' if there ever was one, and a most fastidious person, wrote scathingly of 'the Beefs', the gross overfed squires who drank and snored at his father's colossal country-seat of Houghton in Norfolk; but on the whole it is to the aristocracy that we must ascribe the high level of taste already mentioned. They may have been complacent and conservative, they may have hated 'enthusiasm' in all its forms, but they were in some respects the most cultured ruling class we have ever had, and they did know something about art. Many of them had travelled over Europe on the now fashionable 'Grand Tour', which had hardly become common in Evelyn's day a century before, though his Diary is interesting enough. They studied the ruins, purchased Greek statues and Italian paintings to decorate the stately rooms of their 'rural palaces', and were often extremely competent connoisseurs. Famous architects, who owed everything to their patronage, dedicated sumptuous folios to them in terms of nauseating servility, mixing engravings of Roman ruins with ambitious 'projects' of their own between one pair of boards. Servants in those days were ridiculously cheap and absurdly plentiful: they could be expected to work in kitchens situated in damp dark basements or separated from the principal apartments by draughty open colonnades; they could sleep anywhere, in a windowless attic or behind a Roman balustrade. Such were the prevailing social conditions when the vast imposing mansions of the eighteenth century were built.

First on the list in point of time comes Castle Howard, a colossal house in Yorkshire, erected between 1699 and 1714 for the Earl of Carlisle by Vanbrugh assisted by Nicholas Hawksmoor, a pupil of Wren. Sir John Vanbrugh (1664–1726) is one of the most extraordinary figures in the whole history of architecture. Of Flemish descent, he 'studied' (possibly architecture) in France, joined the army in 1686 and, after a mysterious career, was promoted to captain's rank ten years later. About that time, he wrote his first play, which was an immediate success, and became a member of the celebrated Kit-Cat Club. One of his fellow-members, the Earl of Carlisle, was so much impressed by his talents as a draughtsman that in 1699 he commissioned him to design Castle Howard; so this fortunate playwright, at thirty-five years of age, bought a French edition of Palladio from his bookseller and plunged into architecture with the most startling results. Successful as a dramatist, he was most successful as an architect when he was building something big and dramatic: that is why Castle Howard and Blenheim Palace illustrate his qualities so admirably. The former mansion is enormous, and so formally planned that you can look through the keyholes of the whole sequence of vast state-rooms from end to end of the main block. In the centre rises an imposing dome, very effective from a distance externally, but too lofty within. Walls and floors of the corridors, as of the central hall under the dome, are of smooth stone.

Wren, as we have seen (p. 153), had been influenced by the Baroque movement in Italy but never captured by it. Vanbrugh, the leading Baroque architect in England, designed in a manner all his own, but it was as an exponent of Baroque splendour and dramatic appeal that he excelled rather than in any slavish imitation of Italian Baroque models. Castle Howard was a huge house, even if never so large as he had intended, but it was actually surpassed by Blenheim with its four acres of roof. Blenheim Palace was erected, as every schoolboy knows, by royal command as a gift from the nation to John Churchill, Duke of Marlborough, in token of gratitude for his victory at Blenheim in Bavaria. The story of its building is comic and tragic by turns from start to finish.

Its total frontage, including the wings, is about 850 feet as compared with some 700 feet at Castle Howard, and the house proper is 350 feet wide. The great hall is 67 feet high; and here too it is claimed that you can see through the keyholes of all the twelve large rooms on the garden front, 350 feet from end to end! Stables were provided for scores of horses, but not on the scale of Chantilly in France, built about the same time, where elephants could easily have been accommodated. It has been said of Vanbrugh, acutely rather than unkindly, that he was 'obsessed by the gigantic'; but in creating a building intended as a national monument to a hero rather than as a mere dwelling-house, he displayed his genius. Blenheim is not simply a vulgar pile: it may repel us in this present age of austerity, but as an architectural composition it is superb as well as (intentionally) ostentatious. The famous bridge across the tiny brook that flows near the palace, dammed to form a lake, is all in keeping, with over thirty perfectly useless rooms hidden in its masonry. The human interest in the building of Blenheim, however, rests in the acrimonious correspondence and interviews between Vanbrugh and the Duchess of Marlborough, which lasted over twenty years while her eminently pacific and good-natured husband was away at the wars. All this may be read in Winston Churchill's great biography of his ancestor.

Nicholas Hawksmoor or Hawksmore (1661–1736), who assisted Vanbrugh at Blenheim and had previously been employed by Wren, is generally regarded as the other leading exponent of Baroque architecture in England; and his building where that style is most evident is Queen's College at Oxford (c. 1700–33), including the monumental screen-wall on the High Street (Fig. 45). It will be noticed that this is a very formal and Roman composition, and that neither in the screen-wall itself nor in the buildings at either end of it is there any superabundance of ornament such as is commonly associated with Baroque architecture. It is, however, very boldly conceived for the sole purpose of dramatic effect and has no utilitarian aim: therein lies the reason for Sacheverell Sitwell's recent dictum that it is 'absolutely Baroque in spirit'.

James Gibbs (1682–1754), who also built two famous London churches (p. 167), had studied in Rome under the Baroque architects there. He left his mark on Oxford in the shape of the Radcliffe Library (or 'Camera'), a really magnificent domed building, standing cheek-by-jowl with some of the finest late Gothic architecture of Oxford

45. QUEEN'S COLLEGE, OXFORD

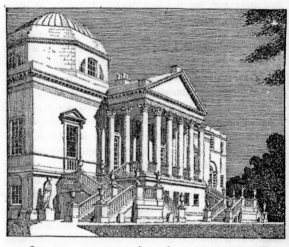

46. CHISWICK HOUSE (THE 'PALLADIAN VILLA')

and yet, somehow, not clashing with it. Some critics have found technical defects in the design of the building, objecting that the plinth is too low and the rotunda too high, but these strictures seem rather captious. At Cambridge, Gibbs built the beautiful Senate House in 1722–30. He also published more than one book on architecture, i.e. on revived Roman architecture. Other architects of this period who must not be forgotten are George Dance who designed the Mansion House in London (1739–45); Giacomo Leoni the designer of Moor Park in Hertfordshire (1720); Colin Campbell who built the colossal Houghton Hall for Sir Robert Walpole (1722–38) and also published a bulky folio, ominously entitled *Vitruvius Britannicus*; and Henry Flitcroft (1697–1769) whose chief claim to fame is Wentworth Woodhouse in Yorkshire, 600 feet long.

Inevitably, mention of Flitcroft recalls that great dilettante and patron of the arts, the third Earl of Burlington (1695–1748), inseparably connected with the name of his protégé and friend William Kent (1684–1748), and also with Flitcroft just mentioned. Burlington was a typical product of his age, a nobleman who had duly made the 'Grand Tour' and, while doing so, had contracted a violent passion for the architectural work of Palladio, which had fallen into eclipse during the time of Wren. In Italy, too, he picked up Kent, a young man of great ability who had been sent to Italy to study by some wealthy patrons. Burlington brought Kent home to London with him in 1716, and lodged him at his house in Piccadilly for the rest of his life. Their first task was the embellishment, on Palladian principles, of that still famous building; but subsequent alterations and additions have greatly modified the original effect.

Burlington and Kent, between them, then proceeded to erect the so-called 'Palladian Villa', more correctly Chiswick House (Fig. 46) in 1730. The design for this was based upon Palladio's celebrated Villa Capra near Vicenza. It is now the property of the Brentford and Chiswick Town Council, and is used as a municipal art-gallery. It is still surrounded by attractive gardens, and on a sunny day it recalls perfectly the line of now shabby villas along the River Brenta where Venetian gallants used to frolic in the gay but artificial days of Tiepolo and Goldoni. There is nothing English about it. The joyous and delicate decoration of the interior shows Kent at his best. He could and did design anything: not only these great houses with their furniture, but ladies' dresses and even the gorgeous state barge now exhibited at the Victoria and Albert Museum. He was also a competent painter and book-illustrator. Among his chief buildings are Holkham in Norfolk, a colossal mansion, and the Horse Guards in Whitehall.

Apart from these fashionable circles in London, there were at least two important schools of provincial architecture in England in the eighteenth century. 'Carr of York' (1723–1807) created an enormous practice among the landed aristocracy of Yorkshire and left an immense fortune at his death, although he began life as a humble mason. Presumably he derived most of his knowledge from books, and he followed the prevailing Palladian fashion without any regard for local tradition. His best-known building is Harewood House (1760), erected for Lord Lascelles and afterwards embellished by Robert Adam. At Buxton he built the Royal Crescent.

Another Yorkshireman, John Wood (c. 1705–54), migrated as a young man to Bath at a fortunate moment for himself, as that famous spa was just then becoming fashionable, partly owing to royal patronage but mainly because of the energetic organizing work of 'Beau Nash', who had joined hands with an able speculator and quarry-owner, Ralph Allen. Of this trio, Nash provided the ideas and the drive, Allen the money and the stone, Wood the imaginative ability which has made Bath one of the most beautiful cities in England. Wood started to build Queen Square in 1728, laid out several streets, and began the erection of the Crescent and the Circus, which were finished by his son after his death; and finally he designed Prior Park (1737–41), Ralph Allen's noble mansion which overlooks the city. Bath is often cited as an example of town-planning, and its lay-out was certainly very fine, but it did not constitute town-planning as we now understand the term, because it did not provide for all social classes or for industry.

In the third quarter of the eighteenth century, the outstanding figure was Robert Adam (1728–92), an able and exceedingly pushful architect educated at Edinburgh University, who attracted attention by the publication of a book of drawings of Diocletian's late Roman palace at Spalato in Dalmatia, and rapidly built up an extensive and lucrative practice. Among the huge houses that he built were Syon House at Isleworth, Kedleston near Derby, and Kenwood at Hampstead; besides many town houses and other buildings too numerous to mention here. With his architect-brothers he laid out the group of streets known as the 'Adelphi' (*adelphoi* in Greek = brothers), now mostly destroyed, though the headquarters of the Royal Society of Arts still remains to indicate his taste in design. He had a commercial interest in a patent stucco, and one of the features of the delicate late Roman or Hellenistic or Pompeian decoration which distinguishes all his work is his masterly use of that material, treated in dainty colours. Adam contrived to design the furniture and carpets of his lordly apartments: excellent examples of his interiors are the library at Kenwood and various rooms at Osterley Park, now both open to the public.

Sir William Chambers (1726–96) goes down to posterity as the architect of Somerset House with its magnificent but now modified frontage to the Thames; but is still more noteworthy for his introduction of Chinese fashions into architecture as a result of his experiences in the Far East as a supercargo in boyhood. The most obvious evidence of this is the Chinese pagoda in Kew Gardens (c. 1760); but books, as usual, served as stepping-stones, and he soon attained Court favour. Chippendale the cabinet-maker introduced *chinoiserie* into his designs, and Chinese wallpapers came into favour. Even French Rococo had its influences on English decoration in the latter part of the century; but on the whole, Chambers remained resolutely Palladian in his architecture and wrote a most Roman and orthodox book about it. Last of the eighteenth-century giants was Sir John Soane (1753–1837), who designed the Bank of England and bequeathed his house in Lincoln's Inn Fields to the nation as a museum. In his collections housed there his catholic taste is evident: all was fish that came into his discriminating net, and his buildings show the influence of Greek as well as of Roman architecture, perhaps as a result of the publication of Stuart and Revett's book *The Antiquities of Athens* in 1762.

Thus we have witnessed a gradual drifting away from the strictly Roman tradition which had governed English architecture for a century and a half. Pompeian, Chinese, and Greek fashions in turn had percolated into our country; and finally the clock was pushed still further back when Napoleon, after his conquest of Egypt in 1798, ordered the publication of the sumptuous folios known as *The Description of Egypt*, which first infected France (the 'Directoire style') and then led Englishmen to borrow details of costume and decoration from the tombs of the Pharaohs. Almost at the same time, 'Prinny', as the Prince Regent was irreverently nicknamed, proceeded to bedeck his charming Georgian house at Brighton with absurd and hideous domes, minarets, and what-not, in a style which he conceived to be Oriental but which was in fact simply barbarous; the appalling result still remains in large part.

But the worst is yet to tell. Superimposed upon all these kaleidoscopic efforts to divert the course of architecture at the end of the eighteenth century came the Gothic Revival. Its genesis is to be seen so far back as Batty Langley's attempt to classify Gothic into 'Orders' (1742), and still more in Horace Walpole's pinchbeck mock-Gothic villa at Strawberry Hill, but its effects had hardly made themselves felt by 1820, the date where this chapter ends, so the Revival is treated in Chapter 12.

The Church of England during the reigns of the first three Georges was, as has been said previously, inactive if tolerant; and the few buildings of any note erected by it during the century are mainly the result of Queen Anne's order for additional London churches, in 1711. They include St. Mary-le-Strand (1714–27) and St. Martin's-in-the-Fields (1722, not one of Anne's fifty) by James Gibbs; St. Mary Woolnoth (1713–19) and St. George's, Bloomsbury (1720–30) by Hawksmoor; and

St. John's, Westminster (1728) by Thomas Archer, who also designed St. Philip's, now the Cathedral, at Birmingham (1711–19). There is another typical example at Blandford in Dorset (*c.* 1735); thereafter the field is almost barren. All these churches are of Roman type, very 'Protestant' in plan as Wren recommended, with internal galleries, Georgian details, and no 'Popish' trappings. They nearly all possess steeples, often in Wren's picturesque manner, sometimes really beautiful (e.g. at St. Martin's-in-the-Fields), sometimes almost hideous (e.g. at St. George's, Bloomsbury). Nonconformist chapels of the eighteenth century resembled them very closely, but were usually more cheaply built and furnished, as no State aid was available towards their cost. When Wesley started his evangelizing campaign he did not intend to sever himself from the mother Church, but, when he was reluctantly compelled to do so, he built the first Methodist chapel (the 'New Room' in the Horsefair at Bristol) in 1739, and the large 'Wesley's Chapel' in City Road, London, in 1777, on the same plan. Both are still standing. Neither Anglicans nor Nonconformists built any neo-Gothic churches before *c.* 1820.

CHAPTER 12

'THE BATTLE OF THE STYLES'
(1820–1900)

RIDICULE OF the nineteenth century has been far too rife for forty years or more. Elegant writers with a gift of words have made a hobby of destroying established reputations, until we are driven to protest that the leaders in Victorian politics, literature, science, and art—even the much maligned Sir Gilbert Scott—were giants in their several fields. Nevertheless, it is difficult to write with any enthusiasm of the general history of English architecture during the century, in spite of many great buildings which it produced. Architecture floundered hopelessly, and oscillated from side to side. 'The Battle of the Styles' was a term coined by Lord Palmerston when he was arguing with Sir Gilbert Scott on the respective merits of Gothic and Palladian design for the new Government buildings, in or about 1859 (p. 178) ; but the battle had begun long before that, and it lasted with little respite till the end of the century. The period has been called with equal justice 'The Age of Revivals', and that title might have been used here, had not the whole Renaissance, from 1550 onwards, been a revival of Roman architecture.

The date 1820 has been chosen as a starting-point because, at that time or thereabouts, the Gothic Revival began to add to the confusion which the introduction of French, Chinese, Pompeian, Greek, and Egyptian elements had produced, as previously explained, in the

169   M

comparatively regular development of the Roman tradition. It was in 1820 that a so-called 'Gothic' church —St. Luke's, Chelsea—was built, for the first time, with one or two exceptions—after an interval of some 270 years. It is a rather poor thing, a Georgian galleried affair clad in feeble medieval trappings, lacking in everything that gives Gothic its virility and charm. Yet it broke the long Roman spell and led to the deluge. Horace Walpole's ludicrous efforts in pinchbeck Gothic at Strawberry Hill (p. 167), a dilettante's plaything, had led nowhere; and the squalid and tawdry little Chapel of St. Peter at Winchester, built in 1792 and illustrated by Sir Kenneth Clark in his entertaining history of the Gothic Revival, is no more than a straw to indicate the direction of the coming gale of medievalism.

In 1820, the Gothic Revival began to compete with the 'Regency' period of Roman architecture associated with 'Prinny', not merely because he was the Regent but also because of his intense personal interest in architecture. John Nash, his capable if rather vulgar architect, had carried out for him many far more pleasing designs than the mock-Saracenic Pavilion at Brighton (p. 167). Chief among them was the great scheme of monumental town-planning between St. James's Park and St. John's Wood in London. Facing St. James's Park he built Carlton House Terrace, with its fine central flight of steps; then Waterloo Place, where the United Services Club is, from his designs, but not the Athenaeum Club opposite; then Regent Street with its magnificent Quadrant; then Langham Place with All Souls' Church; then (north of Portland Place) he laid out Park Crescent; and finally he planned the whole of 'The Regent's Park', with its surrounding terraces of large houses, severely

47. THE ATHENAEUM CLUB, LONDON (1830),
BEFORE ALTERATION

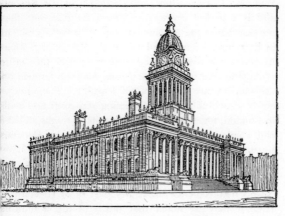

48. LEEDS TOWN HALL (1858)

damaged by enemy action during the 1939–45 war. He also planned Trafalgar Square and built Buckingham Palace (much altered since) and the Marble Arch. Nash had a large practice in addition to this important work for the Crown, but it is for the Regent's great scheme, carried out between 1813 and 1828, that he will be remembered. Regent Street has now been entirely rebuilt, but its original gracious stucco dignity will still be recalled by older readers, and his architecture generally was a sober, competent blend of Graeco-Roman elements, well suited to the needs of his day. There was enough of Greek in it to justify his inclusion among the 'Greek Revivalists'; but he was not immune from the insidious attraction of the new Gothic craze, and indeed built himself a 'Moorish Castle' near Cowes in 1800, with battlements and a castellated conservatory.

The Athenaeum Club (1827–30, Fig. 47) stands on Waterloo Place, within Nash's scheme for the Regent, and is a perfect example of fitness for purpose: that purpose being the accommodation of 'persons eminent in literature, science, and the arts'. Everything about its exterior is dignified and academic; and the statue of Athene, the Panathenaic frieze, and the tripods on the balcony are symbolical of learning. The interior contains one of the most imposing staircases and halls in London, together with a noble suite of rooms and the club's splendid library. It was designed by Decimus Burton, who also built the fine stone screen at Hyde Park Corner, the Roman triumphal arch at the top of Constitution Hill, probably a number of houses in Nash's new Regent's Park, and part of St. Leonard's. Here it may be noted that much of the admirable 'Regency' architecture of Brighton, Weymouth, and

Cheltenham is of approximately the same style and period.

The most definitely Greek architecture of the Greek Revival is to be found in and around Bloomsbury in London. St. Pancras Church (1819–22), by H. W. Inwood, is an extraordinary pastiche of ancient Greek buildings including the caryatid porch of the Erechtheion. Outside Euston Station is a huge Doric propylaeum by Philip Hardwick, and most of the other excellent architecture of the 'London and Birmingham Railway' (now the L.M.S.R.), dating from the eighteen-thirties, is in the same style. The National Gallery (1832–8), by William Wilkins, would probably have been much more Greek if the architect had not been hampered by his instructions. As it stands, it is an ignoble design, far inferior to his fine University College in Gower Street (1828) which, in spite of a Roman portico and the small dome over it, is predominantly Greek in feeling, as is his Downing College at Cambridge (1820). Oxford possesses a splendid example of Greek Revivalism, utterly foreign to the whole spirit of the place, in the Taylor-Randolph Institution, best known as the home of the Ashmolean Museum. This exotic building was designed by S. P. Cockerell, a learned professor who also erected a number of austere Greek banks.

The British Museum (1823–47), by Sir Robert Smirke, is the last important building which is all Greek; and after 1850 the Greek Revival had run its course, except in the work of 'Greek Thomson', who built a number of fine Presbyterian churches of that style in Glasgow between 1850 and 1875. At Cambridge, the Fitzwilliam Museum (1845), by Basevi, is Roman rather than Greek; as is the magnificent St. George's Hall at Liverpool (1815–47). Both these buildings depend largely for their effect upon porticoes with Corinthian columns; but Sir Charles Barry, best known as one of the leaders of the Gothic Revival, introduced a very different note into London with his Travellers' Club (1830) and Reform Club next door (1837), where his exteriors were 'astylar' (i.e. without columns), and were based upon two famous Italian palaces of the Renaissance. Like the adjoining Athenaeum, both these clubs contain splendid interiors, as does his Bridgewater House (1849); but perhaps the most stately interior of all is at his Stafford House, now Lancaster House, of which Queen Victoria is said to have remarked to its ducal owner that she always felt, when she entered it, that she was coming from her cottage to his palace.

The Roman style, usually with a Corinthian colonnade, continued in favour almost to the end of the nineteenth century for municipal buildings. Among these Leeds Town Hall (Fig. 48), built in 1853–8 by Cuthbert Brodrick, is more striking than most, and its cupola is certainly not of orthodox Roman type. The sooty atmosphere of the city considerably detracts from the building's charms. Towards the end of the century, many important neo-Roman municipal buildings were erected, to which reference will be made later; but now we must retrace our steps to trace the parallel course of the Gothic Revival from 1820 onwards.

The history of that movement has been most learnedly and wittily told by Sir Kenneth Clark in 300 pages; but here barely seven pages can be devoted to it: far too little, for personalities, prejudices, and violent passions conspire to make it the most lively period in all our architectural history. Let us begin by taking stock of the position in 1820. As previously observed, hardly any Gothic churches had been built between 1550 and 1820; and such necessary alterations to existing Gothic cathedrals and churches as had been undertaken, from Wren to Wyatt, were amusing rather than edifying efforts. James Wyatt (1746–1813) is sometimes called 'The Destroyer', but was not quite so black as he is painted. He also built two enormous new Gothic mansions: Fonthill Abbey (1796) with an octagonal tower and spire 276 feet high and a hall 120 feet high; and Ashridge Park. The former collapsed in 1825, the latter is still standing.

A taste for the morbid and horrific in literature had produced the 'Gothic romance' about the beginning of the century, with a prevailing atmosphere of ruin, decay, bats, owls, and ivy. Sir Walter Scott's novels, with their emphasis on the chivalry of the Middle Ages, came soon afterwards (1814–32). Close upon their heels followed the Oxford Movement initiated by Keble in 1833, leading to increased interest in the sacraments and ritual of the Church of England. It was the cumulative effect of these and various other influences, rather than any mere swing of the pendulum of architectural taste, that led to the Gothic Revival. Almost simultaneously came a spate of books to furnish intending Gothic architects with ammunition, including *An Attempt to Discriminate the Gothic Styles* (1819), written, rather surprisingly, by a Nonconformist amateur; and *Specimens of Gothic Architecture* (1821) by Augustus Pugin the Elder.

Although the first products of the movement were churches, from 1820 onwards, the results were disappointing for the first two decades or so. In spite of the books then available, the churches erected between 1820 and 1840 were cheap imitations of Gothic, executed with inferior materials and lacking the solidity and constructional vigour that characterized our medieval building. St. Dunstan's-in-the-West (1831) in Fleet Street, based on the design of 'Boston Stump', is at least picturesque. Nevertheless, the movement had made such strides within fifteen years that, when the Palace of Westminster was burnt down in October 1834, it was decided to inaugurate a competition for its rebuilding in 'the Gothic or Elizabethan styles'. Among the ninety-seven competitors for this great prize, Charles Barry was successful with a superb plan in late Gothic dress. His name has already been mentioned (p. 174) as the designer of two famous clubs in Pall Mall, both in the Italian manner; yet on this occasion he had contrived to assimilate, mainly from books, a profound knowledge of Gothic, and he wisely chose the 'Perpendicular' phase as being most appropriate to his purpose. Opinions still differ as to the result: many critics who may feel bound to disparage the design in public, lest they be thought out-of-date, probably cherish a secret admiration for it in their hearts; and very few people who study the whole group from the Victoria Tower Gardens, from Parliament Square, or from the other side of the river, dare deny that it is a masterpiece. Internally, it is equally impressive, and the way in which Barry has contrived to amalgamate the old Westminster Hall and St. Stephen's Chapel into his new building is very skilful.

Like nearly all his contemporaries, Barry had travelled abroad as a young man, Europe now being open after the Napoleonic wars. Unlike them, however, he had not confined his attention to Greece and Italy; indeed, he spent only a fortnight in Greece. Admittedly he ignored the medieval buildings of Rouen, but later in his tour he did take some interest in Gothic architecture. Yet when he found himself commissioned to rebuild the Palace of Westminster he felt the need of some expert in medieval craftsmanship to assist him; so he wisely chose Augustus Welby Northmore Pugin, son of that elder Augustus who had produced some of the first albums of drawings of Gothic detail. Welby Pugin worked loyally and industriously with Barry at Westminster and deserves much of the credit for the splendid craftsmanship of all kinds in that noble building. He was a most religious man, an ardent Roman Catholic, and many tales are told of his eccentric habits.

The outstanding figure of the Gothic Revival, Sir Gilbert Scott (1810-77), earned an almost legendary reputation. He was in no way eccentric, but a very hard-headed and successful practitioner of great ability. He spent his earlier years slaving with furious energy at the building of workhouses and then of cheap Gothic churches, for which he afterwards confessed a sense of shame. He seems to have been converted to the real nature of Gothic by Welby Pugin about 1840, and in 1844 he won an international competition for a new Lutheran cathedral at Hamburg, after a lightning tour of Germany when he visited and sketched a cathedral a day. This success appears to have been the cause of his appointment to restore one cathedral after another. In that connexion, his name has become a by-word, and it is commonly believed that his work consisted of wholesale destruction and the elimination of every historical feature that did not match his favourite mid-Gothic style. There is a measure of truth in that view: his restorations were drastic and wholesale; he did replace mellow old furnishings with shiny, gaudy substitutes which, even if they were accurate reproductions of medieval prototypes, were lamentably lacking in restful restraint. On the other hand, he was conservative compared with some of his contemporaries, he saved several cathedrals from collapse by his thorough knowledge of medieval construction, and his knowledge of Gothic architecture in general was prodigious.

For so able and learned a man, he was, however, far too complacent about his own designs. The Albert Memorial (1862–72) is almost universally regarded as a tasteless if not an actually hideous monument on a regrettably large scale. He became a leading protagonist in 'The Battle of the Styles' which ensued after he had won another great competition in 1858 for the new Government offices in Whitehall (including the present Foreign Office), when he vanquished 218 rivals. Characteristically, he wrote afterwards that his own drawings were 'probably the best ever sent in to a competition'. But his design was Gothic, and Lord Palmerston wanted Italian Renaissance. After a most unedifying squabble among politicians and architects, in and out of Parliament, Scott finally relinquished the martyr's crown that he might have earned by sticking to his Gothic principles, and capitulated in 1861, naïvely observing that 'to resign would be to give up a sort of property which Providence had placed in the hands of my family'. It is not surprising that he left a fortune of £120,000 at his death, or that he had been connected with 730 buildings during the last thirty years of his life. They included many excellent churches

49. THE UNIVERSITY MUSEUM, OXFORD (1860)

50. 'GRIM'S DYKE', HARROW WEALD (1872)

(e.g. at Ealing, Kensington, Halifax, and St. Mary's Cathedral at Edinburgh), as well as Glasgow University, and St. Pancras Station (1865) which is often bracketed with the Albert Memorial as his worst large design.

In the competition for the Law Courts in 1866, Scott's Gothic design was unsuccessful, and G. E. Street was awarded the premium, but building did not begin till 1874. This excessively picturesque composition proved an utter failure from a functional point of view, and general recognition of that fact marked the end of the Gothic Revival for public buildings. Alfred Waterhouse's Assize Courts (1864) and Town Hall (1868) at Manchester are other examples of its last phase. It was now realized at long last that traceried windows do not provide the best means of lighting public offices or hospitals, and that crocketed pinnacles are not essential to the efficient transaction of municipal affairs.

For churches, however—not only Anglican and Roman Catholic but Nonconformist too—Gothic continued to be regarded as the only 'Christian' way of building, and often the results were deplorable, especially where funds were inadequate to allow medieval features to be aped successfully or where the architect employed did not apprehend the true nature of Gothic. Polychrome decoration derived from Venice and northern France, thanks to Ruskin's books, was too freely introduced: notably by William Butterfield in his gaudy interiors of All Saints, Margaret Street (1850), and St. Alban's, Holborn (1860); also in the chapel and other buildings of Keble College (1870), which is altogether out of place in Oxford. The best churches of the last years of the nineteenth century are by G. F. Bodley and by J. L. Pearson, whose Truro Cathedral (1887–1910, Fig. 51) is a really superb and scholarly design in every respect, but quite French and as exotic in Cornwall as Keble is at Oxford, even if a trifle less blatant.

This fondness for alien Gothic features must be attributed partly to the fact that English architects now habitually roamed over western Europe, filling their sketch-books with picturesque medieval tit-bits instead of concentrating upon laborious measured drawings of Greek and Roman ruins; and partly to John Ruskin, who published *The Seven Lamps of Architecture* in 1849 and *The Stones of Venice* in 1851–3. His 'fatal gifts of enthusiasm and eloquence', to quote Sir Kenneth Clark's words, did as much harm as good to the art he so genuinely loved; and his admirable gospel of sincerity in construction only bore fruit in the later work of William Morris and C. F. A. Voysey (pp. 184, 185-6). He became a dictator in all matters of taste, educated England hanging on his words; and his obsession with sculptured detail, coupled with his infatuation for French and Venetian rather than English architecture, led many of his admirers astray. His dogmatic and violent views on 'the foul torrent of the Renaissance' are well known, but his passionate advocacy of social reform made little impression upon an age which witnessed the creation of so many slums. Finally, the Oxford Museum (Fig. 49), in the building of which he took so prominent a part, is a negation of all his artistic teaching, and is universally regarded to-day as one of the ugliest buildings in that lovely city. The Great Exhibition of 1851 displayed English industrial design at its nadir, but the 'Crystal

Palace' in which it was housed will come in for mention
in the next chapter.

The reader will have noticed that nothing has been
said hitherto of domestic architecture between 1820 and
1870, the point we have now reached. Naturally, houses
large and small were built throughout that period, and
many of them were Gothic of a sort, to the extent of
reproducing scraps of carved medieval ornament in
moulded cast-iron, terracotta, and cement. Designs
started from architects' sketch-books, and each fleeting
fashion reached the speculative builder about a generation after the architect himself had discarded it. The
origin of nearly every 'decorative' feature on suburban
villas which critics have scarified in withering letters to
the Press can be found in some architect's holiday tour
in Flanders, Normandy, or Venice; and it only became
unspeakably vulgar after it had passed out of fashion.

Consider, for example, the house at Harrow Weald
(Fig. 50) which Norman Shaw, R.A., designed for
another famous Academician—a painter—in 1872.
Shaw was a most accomplished architect, one of the
Victorian giants, and he designed to order in any
required style—admirable late Gothic in a church at
Ilkley (1878), 'Queen Anne' in Queen's Gate (1888),
free and florid Roman Renaissance at the Piccadilly
Hotel (1905), and all varieties of Tudor or Jacobean as
his fancy, or his client's fancy, took him. The house
illustrated doubtless raises derision among the young of
to-day, nurtured in extreme austerity; yet it is a far
more honest design than most of its period and is well
built. Norman Shaw, who had an immense practice,
did in fact learn much from the movement launched

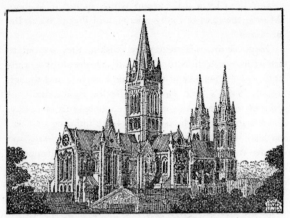

51. TRURO CATHEDRAL (1887–1910)

52. LIVERPOOL CATHEDRAL (1904–)

about 1860 by a little group which included William
Morris, the man of many talents, and Philip Webb the
architect.

Inspired to some degree by Ruskin, they set out to
free English architecture and all the decorative crafts
from the artificiality of the Gothic Revival; and though
Philip Webb's 'Red House' at Bexley Heath, built for
Morris in 1859, seems ordinary enough to us of to-day,
it set a standard of honest direct brick building that was
to lead to greater things. One merit of this 'Arts and
Crafts' movement was that it endeavoured to strengthen
the *English* tradition. Norman Shaw and Sir Ernest
George were the two most distinguished house-designers
of the late nineteenth century. In George's office were
trained, among many others, Sir Guy Dawber and Sir
Edwin Lutyens, who carried on his style, modified and
much simplified, into the present century (p. 186).
About 1900, the larger houses, whether in town or
country, were somewhat florid; but their windows were
at least free from tracery, and their pleasant aspect was
prevailingly English in spite of curly Flemish gables and
a good deal of terracotta. So far as they can be labelled,
they were neo-Tudor or neo-Jacobean.

CHAPTER 13

TWENTIETH-CENTURY ARCHITECTURE IN ENGLAND (1900–1939)

THE TWENTIETH century has already witnessed a complete change in the character of our architecture, not only in the type of buildings erected but also in their form. This change is due primarily, of course, to the drastic effect of the two great wars of 1914–18 and 1939–45, and it occurred in the period between them; but there were other events, such as the influx of refugee-architects from Germany and Austria in the nineteen-thirties, which, as we shall see, exerted an important influence on design. In the circumstances prevailing at the time of writing (1946), when the building trade is still paralysed as a result of the second world-war and our concern is mainly to provide a large number of cottages for our millions of homeless or inadequately housed people, it is undesirable to attempt to carry the story beyond 1939. This chapter, therefore, naturally divides itself into two distinct periods: from 1900 to 1914 and from 1919 to 1939.

In 1900, Gothic churches and 'free Classic' public buildings were still being erected, but something like a revolution in the design of dwelling-houses had been brought about by one man, C. F. A. Voysey (1857–1941), whose charming home at Chorley Wood, built in 1900, is illustrated in Fig. 53. To modern eyes, this house may appear consciously picturesque, 'olde worlde', and archaic; but in its simplicity and its honesty of

construction it affords a welcome relief from the obvious
'period design' of Grim's Dyke (Fig. 50), a generation
earlier; its interior, too, is dainty and restful. At the
turn of the century, Voysey was building similar houses
in scores all over England, with steep roofs and gables,
low rooms, small mullioned windows with leaded lights,
and black chimney-pots. His example was soon followed
by other architects; and in 1904–5 Muthesius, a German
critic, published a book, *Das Englische Haus*, in which
English domestic architecture was lauded to the skies,
with a great effect in foreign countries. Another English,
or rather Scottish, designer, who is sometimes associated
with Voysey as a pioneer, was C. R. Mackintosh, but his
output was small, and in my view his influence was much
less, though he did cause the Germans to coin the
appalling word 'Mackintoshismus'. Apart from Voysey,
the leading architects of country-houses at this period
were Sir Edwin Lutyens, Sir Guy Dawber, and Ernest
Newton. All three followed in the tradition of Sir
Ernest George (p. 184); but their houses were less
ornate in detail, and Lutyens in particular developed a
style all his own—simple but very expensive. In 1900,
every period of English historical design had been ex-
haustively described and illustrated in elaborate books,
and for the larger houses it was generally a case of de-
ciding which 'period' style to choose—Elizabethan,
Tudor, Georgian, or what-not—but never Gothic.
Voysey broke this spell to a considerable extent; and
next came a welcome improvement in the design of small
houses and cottages, hitherto left far too much to the
tender mercies of the speculative builder.

Before 1900, very little attention had been paid
to these minor dwellings, though a few enlightened

53. 'THE ORCHARD', CHORLEYWOOD (1900):
C. F. A. VOYSEY'S OWN HOUSE

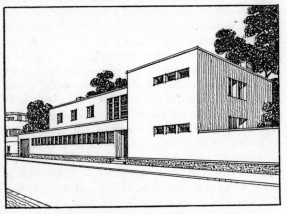

54. HOUSE IN CHURCH STREET, CHELSEA:
BY MENDELSOHN AND CHERMAYEFF

employers had laid out 'model villages' for their people: of these the chief examples were Port Sunlight (1888 onwards) for Mr. W. H. Lever, afterwards Lord Leverhulme; and Bournville near Birmingham (1895 onwards) for Messrs. Cadbury Bros. These settlements were far ahead of anything that had preceded them, in the provision of communal amenities and a tasteful lay-out as well as in the actual design of the houses. In 1898 an obscure and impecunious Press reporter named Ebe-nezer Howard published a book, *Tomorrow*, republished in 1902 as *Garden Cities of Tomorrow*, in which he lit a torch that is now burning more brightly than ever. His thesis, simply but most convincingly expounded, was that modern cities are far too ugly and far too big, that their inhabitants are divorced from the health-giving country and have to travel excessive distances from home to work. He therefore advocated the 'Garden City', artificially and attractively planned round a civic centre, provided with all amenities, with sufficient industry to employ all the citizens, and surrounded by a 'green belt' of agricul-tural land owned by the community and capable of supplying them with milk and produce as well as with fresh air. This belt would prevent the outward spread of the urban area, for which Howard suggested, as an ideal, a population of 32,000, i.e. large enough to carry a reasonable load of civic amenities, but small enough to possess the advantages of a country town.

Howard's book very soon bore fruit. The 'First Garden City Ltd.' was established at Letchworth in 1903, designed by Raymond Unwin and Barry Parker. For seventeen years it remained without a rival; and, although a second Garden City was established at Welwyn in 1920, no others have followed. Yet all our town planning experts agree that there is no alternative better than Howard's idea and Unwin's plan. For, in spite of Regent Street and Bath and Port Sunlight and Bournville, this was the first attempt to establish a complete community on scientific and artistic lines, entirely self-contained, with its own industries, its civic amenities, and—above all—its agricultural belt. In 1909, Unwin, who combined great practical ability and imagination with his ideals of social betterment, produced the first manual of the new subject under the title *Town Planning in Practice*. Few people realize that, up to 1906, the familiar term 'town planning' had never been used. Since that not very remote date, town planning has created a whole vocabulary of technical jargon, a crop of books, a professional institute holding examinations and granting diplomas, special faculties or schools for its study, and a complete revolution in our social outlook. Both Unwin and Howard richly deserved the knighthoods awarded to them. Suburban estates soon began to benefit by the increased attention paid to the aesthetics of planning, and in 1907 Unwin laid out the Hampstead Garden Suburb. Admirable as that scheme is, it complies in no way with Howard's conception of a Garden City; but it came to be included in the itinerary of numerous pilgrimages made to our island by enthusiasts from abroad who accepted England as *facile princeps* in the new art.

Abreast of these refreshing innovations, uncertainty of purpose prevailed among the designers of public buildings. Apart from architects who continued to favour some form of Roman Renaissance, there was a small group which followed neither Gothic nor orthodox classic lines, and yet failed to produce any enduring improvement in design. T. E. Collcutt was perhaps the most successful practitioner in this field, and though his Imperial Institute in London (1887-93) does display a good deal of fussy hybrid detail, the lofty tower is an original and pleasing feature. Sir Aston Webb, an immensely prosperous architect who received every honour available to members of his profession, created, in the course of a huge practice, an extraordinary group of florid buildings for Birmingham University in 1906-9, and a hardly less exuberant design in the Victoria and Albert Museum, opened with great pomp and circumstance in 1909. In that year, with more pomp, King Edward VII laid the foundation-stone of Webb's new Imperial College of Science hard by, but that is a much less bombastic building. A little earlier than these, Henry T. Hare's Municipal Buildings at Oxford (1893-7) and Sir T. G. Jackson's extensive work at both Oxford and Cambridge were obviously attempts to comply with local tradition by using Elizabethan or Jacobean features and should be judged accordingly.

The chief exponent of 'free Classic' or modified Roman Renaissance architecture in 1900 was John Belcher, a learned and competent architect. His principal works were the Institute of Chartered Accountants and Electra House in the City of London, and his imposing town hall at Colchester (1898-1902). In 1909, Gordon Selfridge invaded London with his famous store in Oxford Street, a building which has been more severely criticized for insincerity of expression than any other modern structure: for that reason, it is comforting to note that it was designed by an American architect, but in 1909 it was hailed as a masterpiece. To this brief list may be added the Central Criminal Court, the War

Office, and the Government buildings at the south end of Whitehall.

Edward VII's short reign was a very splendid and prosperous period when public life in London and social life in its West End reached an outward brilliance that will probably never be seen again. Resulting from this splendour, there was an element of ostentation in some of the buildings mentioned; and even in the hands of Sir Edwin Cooper, a consummate master of design and planning in the 'grand manner', there is a hint of it, e.g. in his magnificent Port of London Building (1912). The competition for the London County Hall was won in 1908 by Ralph Knott at the early age of twenty-eight, with a design which won general admiration at the time and is well suited to its prominent site. But, on the whole, the finest architecture of that opulent period was the great group of buildings in Cathays Park, Cardiff—the City Hall and Law Courts—the result of a competition won by Lanchester and Rickards in 1899 and completed in 1905. As at the Central Hall in Westminster, another competition won by the same firm in 1904, the style adopted was Austrian Baroque, such as one sees in Prague and Vienna, hitherto eschewed by English architects as being vulgar if not indeed 'immoral', for Ruskin's teaching still lingered in the popular mind. Yet in its picturesque grouping and in its general grandeur, this noble group in its monumental setting remains the finest product of Edwardian architecture.

Churches of all denominations continued to be mainly Gothic, and the great new Anglican cathedral at Liverpool (Fig. 52), still incomplete, was begun in 1904 from designs submitted in competition at the early age of twenty-two by Giles Gilbert Scott, grandson of the famous Victorian cathedral-restorer. Himself a pupil of that talented architect G. F. Bodley, he has produced a building of medieval character, yet so original and so well adapted to modern needs that it has been universally praised by critics. The Roman Catholic Cathedral at Westminster, on the other hand, was erected in 1895–1903 in the Byzantine style, by G. F. Bentley, who personally favoured Gothic; but his clients decided otherwise, and so he proceeded to travel in Italy and to Constantinople in order to collect ideas for a church which, though nothing like it had ever been built abroad, admirably fulfils its purpose.

*   *   *

The Great War of 1914–18 put an end to nearly all building operations, though a few incomplete major projects (e.g. Liverpool Cathedral) were continued at half-pressure. With the demobilization of large armies in 1919, there arose a clamant cry for houses in great numbers. An ill-judged slogan, 'Homes for Heroes', soon became the subject of ironical and even bitter jest, for the superhuman efforts made by Government departments, municipal authorities, and architects soon proved insufficient to meet the emergency. Comparing the position in 1919 with that prevailing in 1946, it may be said that, though casualties were heavier in the earlier war, the material damage caused by air-raids and the general upheaval in industry were infinitely less. The new housing-estates eventually built after 1919 showed an advance in lay-out far ahead of anything previously conceived, thanks to the pioneer work of Unwin and Howard in the decade before 1914; and the houses themselves were, for the most, well designed and equipped, though the universal preference for semi-detached dwellings led to an effect of monotony which has since been unfavourably criticized. A second Garden City was established at Welwyn in 1920, on the same lines as at Letchworth, but with various improvements as a result of experience in the earlier venture. The London County Council created some of the best and most attractive housing-schemes; but, in the largest of all, at Becontree in Essex, their huge new town or suburb has been fiercely attacked as a 'one class' artisan community—even as a 'social concentration camp'—lacking many of the civic amenities provided in a 'Garden City' proper. Town planning continued to develop apace all over the country, but has been admirably dealt with by Sir Patrick Abercrombie in another volume of this series, and cannot be given adequate treatment here.

Between 1900 and 1914, as we have seen, architects from Continental Europe came over to England in shoals to study our domestic design, in particular our one 'Garden City' and our so-called 'Garden Suburbs'. They were not interested to the same extent in our 'free-Classic' public buildings or in our neo-Gothic or neo-Byzantine churches. Soon after the first world-war ended in 1918, the tide began to flow in the opposite direction: English architects flocked to the Continent for inspiration. Holland, having preserved its neutrality throughout the war, was able to embark upon large housing-schemes immediately afterwards, while France and England were still recovering their breath and licking their wounds: indeed, Holland had carried out some building of the sort during the actual war years. The leader of the new movement in Holland, when it began some twenty years earlier, was H. P. Berlage, who preached the gospel of truthful construction, arguing that structural elements should be left naked and unashamed; but other inspiration had come from Austria, Germany, and France, where many public, industrial, and even domestic buildings had been erected in a stark untraditional style which heralded a coming revolution in architecture. In Holland, Amsterdam was the centre of the post-war housing drive, and a young architect named Klerk its leader. Before his early death he erected a large number of highly original, very cheap, and somewhat bizarre dwellings for artisans, with brick-faced exteriors and flat roofs. Time dealt hardly with some of the latter, and a demand arose for a return to sloping roofs in future schemes; but he was one of the first architects to persuade English colleagues that flat roofs are essential to modern conditions. Parties of eager architectural students, and sceptical practitioners of more advanced age, were shepherded over to Amsterdam to behold this latest miracle. The excellent work of W. M. Dudok, at Hilversum in particular, was admired by competent English critics. Other conducted tours were made to Germany, Austria, and France, where the pilgrims saw striking designs in reinforced concrete, a very pliable material first used in France but barely known in England in 1900 and clumsily handled by our architects before 1920.

In 1924 appeared a book *Vers une Architecture* (translated into English in 1927), written by a Swiss architect who, for reasons best known to himself, adopted the sobriquet of 'Le Corbusier'. This book had a tremendous vogue among architectural students and young architects in England, already thirsting for a new and revolutionary gospel of building. They swallowed it whole, together with all the designs and all the ideas—some of them patently ridiculous—of the new prophet or soothsayer. It was this book, appearing as it did when the moment was so propitious, that really led to the absurdly-named 'modern' or 'modernist' movement in our architecture, and goaded the venerable but vigorous Sir Reginald Blomfield to publish in 1934 a most amusing volume, ironically entitled *Modernismus*, in which he upheld the traditional position and castigated the upstart doctrine with terrific gusto and obvious enjoyment.

The gospel according to 'Le Corbusier' stresses the importance of function in architecture above everything else: reason must subordinate form to function. He extolled anything and everything built or made by engineers—bridges, aeroplanes, motor-cars, locomotives—on the ground that in each case function dictated form, without superfluous trappings; and he poured scorn upon everything designed by architects. This doctrine spread like wildfire through the English architectural schools, and students tried to jettison everything connected with the past, from Gothic mouldings and tracery to the hated 'Orders'. It seemed that, for them, the whole English tradition had perished in a night. One unexpected result of the new movement was the sudden exhumation of the 'Crystal Palace', a forgotten relic of 1851; ostensibly because it expressed its structure frankly, but possibly also because it was designed by a clever ex-gardener, not by an architect.

Finally, between 1930 and 1939 came a steady trickle of architects from Germany and Austria, many or most of them Jews, political refugees driven out by Hitler, but also including other cosmopolitan immigrants from further east. Some of them stayed in England, others crossed to the United States when the war caught them up, others went to Palestine. Their influence upon the younger members of the profession, especially students, was great; and some of it will assuredly be permanent. The type of architecture favoured by these refugees is represented in England only by scattered examples, some of which will be mentioned here: to see it in the mass, one must go to Haifa or Tel Aviv in Palestine, where it naturally finds its spiritual home.

Most of the new 'modernist' buildings are in reinforced concrete, or in brick covered with cement to simulate concrete, and have sheer white walls devoid of cornices or mouldings. Photographed, as they invariably are, immediately after completion in strong sunlight against a deep blue sky, they look very effective; and in Palestine or on the Riviera strong sunlight is normal, but in our climate they soon look shabby and the cement covering is liable to 'craze' or crack, spoiling the appearance. Roofs are always flat, a method which facilitates planning, as a sloping roof involves a good deal of scheming for the architect; but a flat roof that is badly built is a constant source of trouble and has other disadvantages which seldom arise with the sloping type. Windows are very generously provided, often at the angles of the building; and small panes, which used to be considered an asset for the 'scale' and interest that they give to a building but which entail much work in cleaning and painting, are never used. Excessive glass-area, however, involves much loss of heat in our cold climate, and that fact should be borne in mind, especially when coal is scarce. The interiors of these houses are invariably well planned from a 'functional' and labour-saving aspect, an important point in their favour. The despised drawing-room of Edwardian days, with a separate dining-room, gives place to one large all-purpose 'lounge', a feature which may satisfy gregarious people with no children but which fails under the conditions of normal family life, where one member of the household, at least, often seeks some refuge from the never-ceasing radio in order to work or rest. At their best, houses of this type provide a welcome reaction from the ornamental complexity of the Edwardian home, but most of them have no distinctive national character, and might just as well be located in Prague or Paris or Vienna or Berlin—or Tel Aviv. Whether that cosmopolitan or international impress is, in fact, a defect is a matter for argument; but there are many parts of England where it would clash with the natural surroundings: among the grey villages of the Yorkshire dales or the Cotswolds, for example, or in several other districts which have a marked individuality of their own. Typical specimens of full-blown modernism of this type are the De La Warr Pavilion at Bexhill, the houses at Chelsea illustrated in Fig. 54, the block of flats known as 'Highpoint' at Highgate, the Health Centre at Peckham, the Impington Village College near Cambridge, a group of flats at Ladbroke Grove, and some much discussed houses in Frognal at Hampstead. Advanced modern buildings in brickwork, with flat roofs and large windows, are the Royal Masonic Hospital at Ravenscourt Park, the Burlington School at Hammersmith, the Hornsey Town Hall, and the latest stations of the Underground Railways (now the London Passenger Transport Board); also many of the schools erected between the wars by the Middlesex County Council.

Less revolutionary in character and altogether admirable in design are the Civic Centre at Swansea, the headquarters building of London Transport over St. James's Park Station, and the immense Senate House of London University (Fig. 55), finished in 1939. The last two examples show American influence in the recessing of their upper storeys to comply with 'zoning' restrictions for light and air, and should be compared with Fig. 59.

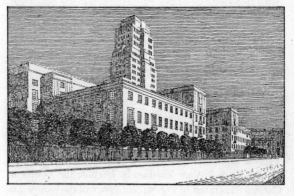

55. LONDON UNIVERSITY: THE SENATE HOUSE

Then there are the splendid but still unfinished buildings of Leeds University, somewhat in the 'grand manner' used for the Cardiff civic centre by the same architects; the picturesque City Hall at Norwich and the new County Hall at Hertford, both displaying Swedish influence; the more conservative Guildhall in Cambridge Market Place; and many other worthy municipal buildings. There are innumerable new blocks of flats in London, where a reasonably modern exterior encloses skilfully planned and equipped interiors; and even cinemas and hotels had begun to shed their superfluous trappings before 1939. Finally, there is Guildford Cathedral, begun in 1938. It will be a noble church, modern in its dignified austerity yet thoroughly Gothic in character, but unfortunately only a small part of it has yet been completed.

*　　　*　　　*

At the present juncture it would be idle to attempt any forecast of the extent to which alien influences will modify or actually extinguish our national tradition. There were many features of our Victorian and Edwardian architecture which were undesirable, vulgar, and redundant: a thorough spring-cleaning was certainly overdue. The danger is that we may drift into mere nihilism, with austerity and mechanical efficiency as our sole watchwords; and, lastly, that in eliminating everything that has graced our buildings of the past we may create new cities which are only a pale replica of the new Moscow or the new Berlin.

CHAPTER 14

ARCHITECTURE IN NORTH AMERICA
SINCE 1620

IF THE Transatlantic reader of these pages should feel
that the space allotted here to the architecture of North
America during the past three centuries is niggardly, he
may be reminded that the first two-thirds of this book
deals with the common heritage of the English-speaking
peoples; and, moreover, that since 1620 American
architecture has closely followed on English lines, all
through the various phases of the later Renaissance and
the subsequent Greek, Gothic, and other revivals. In
this chapter, it will be explained in what respects
American development in this field has resembled or
differed from contemporary movements in England. At
the outset, it must be borne in mind that Spanish and
French settlers occupied parts of the North American
continent before the English arrived, so that some effect
of their national traditions is to be expected on the
architecture of the United States and Canada.

The first English colonists set foot in Virginia in 1607,
and in New England ('the Pilgrim Fathers') in 1620.
The French founded Port Royal (now Annapolis) in
Nova Scotia in 1604, and Québec in 1608, but did not
settle in Louisiana and the Mississippi valley before the
eighteenth century. The Spaniards were earlier in the
field, having established the town of St. Augustine in
Florida in 1565, and Santa Fé (in the modern state of
New Mexico) in c. 1605; while Mexico itself already

contained a great number of their Renaissance and Baroque buildings, some of considerable size and splendour, erected since the days of the conquest in 1521. The Dutch, who had founded their colony of 'New Holland' in 1624, purchased Manhattan Island in 1626 for the extravagant sum of 60 guilders (= *c.* 24 dollars), and by the end of that year had erected thirty bark-covered houses there. This was the beginning of their town of 'New Amsterdam', which became 'New York' when the British occupied it in 1664; and even as late as the mid-eighteenth century it looked remarkably like European Amsterdam with its steep roofs and stepped brick gables. The last vestige of that picturesque sea-faring town was submerged long ago beneath the towering skyscrapers of New York; and survivals of the brief Dutch occupation elsewhere are non-existent or negligible. Even the few features of later architecture ascribed to Holland may equally well have been derived from eastern England, where Dutch influence was always strong. Any remains of Spanish architecture in the states of Florida, New Mexico, and Texas are of slight importance. The charming Spanish 'missions' along the coast of California from San Diego to San Francisco are not so ancient as they appear, having been erected after 1776 by Fra Junipero Serra and other friars.

American buildings of the seventeenth century, regrettably scarce as they are, may therefore be divided into three groups: English in Virginia and New England, French in Canada. It is generally agreed that the oldest building in the United States is the little brick church of St. Luke in Isle of Wight County, Virginia, erected in 1632. To those who think of the U.S.A. as a 'new' country, it may be surprising to learn that St. Luke's is a Gothic church: a belated straggler, no doubt, and very rustic in execution, but Gothic none the less. It has a brick gable with 'corbie-steps', and brick tracery, unusual features characteristic of a corner of Essex in England, where, in my opinion, its prototype—built in 1563-4—may be found in the obscure hamlet of Woodham Walter. Not far from St. Luke's church stands another old building, known as 'Bacon's Castle', and sadly altered since it was originally erected, some time before 1676. It is a brick house of Jacobean type, with splendid chimneys, curved gables and mullioned windows, akin to many surviving examples in the eastern counties of England. Little else of interest remains from the early days of Virginia, where brick was used by the settlers from 1611 onwards.

In the New England states, however, some sixty-five or seventy buildings can be attributed with confidence to the seventeenth century. For the most part they are dwelling-houses, of very simple and uniform character. Stone was fairly abundant, but lime for mortar was scarce, so the use of stone was generally restricted to cellars, plinth-walls, and chimneys. In later work, brick served the same purpose. The whole of the remainder of the structure was of wood, the stout timber framing being covered with 'clap-boards' (weather-boarding) and the roof with thatch at first, later with shingles. In 1930, a restoration was made of the first group of houses erected by the settlers at Salem, Mass., in 1630. These were mere huts of the most primitive type, and the oldest surviving framed house ('The House of the Seven Gables' at Salem) is thought to be not earlier than 1635. The example illustrated (Fig. 56) is the John Ward

56. THE JOHN WARD HOUSE, SALEM, MASS., U.S.A. (*c.* 1684)

57. WESTOVER, VIRGINIA (*c.* 1726)

House at Salem, c. 1684. Other excellent specimens are the 'Scotch House' at Saugus, Mass. (1651); the Hyland-Wildman (c. 1660) and Starr (c. 1645) Houses at Guilford, Conn.; the Older Cowles House at Farmington, Conn. (1650–60); Paul Revere House at Boston, Mass. (c. 1676); Hathaway House at Salem (1682–93); and, best of all, the beautiful Parson Capen House at Topsfield, Mass. (1683). These charming buildings are fully described in my book *The Homes of the Pilgrim Fathers*, where it is argued that their style is directly derived from wooden houses in Essex (England), whence so many of the early settlers came. They are essentially Gothic rather than Classic in style, with steep gables, bold and massive chimneys, mullioned windows with leaded lights—superseded by sash-windows c. 1685. The interiors have batten doors, very large fireplaces, and well designed staircases. Among the considerable number of old churches and meeting-houses in the eastern states, only two seem to be ascribed to the seventeenth century: the 'Old Ship' Church at Hingham, Mass. (1681) and the Old Swedes' Church at Philadelphia (1697–9). They are quaint and typical Puritan meeting-houses like those that were being built in England at the same period.

Although Québec was founded in 1608 and Montréal in 1642, very few buildings of the seventeenth century have survived intact. When the Ursuline Convent was erected in 1642, it was one of the rare stone structures in Québec, the houses of the settlers being of wood. This original wing of the convent still remains as part of the present large group, and was extended before the end of the century, but the fine carved woodwork in the chapel is somewhat later. At Montréal, the McTavish

House dates from *c.* 1650 and the Seminary from 1680. A few of the picturesque little churches in the province, with spires over the west end, are of the same period.

At the turn of the century, the most interesting and beautiful example of historical architecture in the United States came into being. This was the small town of Williamsburg in Virginia, which served as the capital of the colony from 1699 to 1779 but had been settled since 1632. The oldest important building is the William and Mary College (1693–7) of which its first Professor of Mathematics wrote in 1722 that 'the College Building is beautiful and commodious, being first modelled by Sir Christopher Wren, adapted to the nature of the country by the gentlemen there . . . and is not unlike Chelsea Hospital'. As this statement was made within Wren's lifetime, it cannot be disregarded, although there seems to be no other evidence that he was concerned. At all events, it is a charming design and, like Groombridge Place (p. 152), is worthy of his genius even if complete proof be lacking. In 1699 the new capital was laid out on most ambitious lines for so small a place. From the College, a splendid avenue, 'The Palace Green', was constructed, 1,200 feet long and 210 feet wide, with the 'Governor's Palace' at the other end, and with parallel subsidiary streets. The public buildings and church (1717) were of brick, the dwelling-houses mainly of timber. It was a perfect example of the English late Renaissance style, but had fallen into decay when, in 1925, J. D. Rockefeller, junior, was persuaded by the local clergyman to undertake its complete restoration, regardless of expense.

Architects and antiquaries were enlisted to study the former state of the town, and their task was accomplished before the second world-war. A drastic 'purge' of all inharmonious buildings was made, 572 of them were demolished, all the eighteenth-century monuments were restored to their original appearance, and a judicious selection of requisite new buildings (including shops) were designed in the 'Queen Anne' style. The ultimate result, meticulously correct in all details of furniture, decoration, and planting, is one of the loveliest little towns in the world.

During the period 1714–1820, covered by Chapter 11 of this book, American architecture followed surprisingly closely upon the same lines as development in England, although the Declaration of Independence in 1776 naturally severed the colonial connexion between Britain and the United States. English 'copy-books' of classical detail continued to be used freely in America after the separation as before it, and the Georgian era has been defined by one authority as 'the age of books'. Palladio's work was the 'architectural Bible', and the manuals of James Gibbs and others were pored over by builders and carpenters as well as by architects and amateurs. Fig. 57 illustrates one of the finest houses of the early Georgian period, 'Westover' in Virginia, built shortly after 1726. With its dignified yet homely formalism, it resembles the best work of Wren. On the ground floor are four large rooms with a central staircase-hall. The Governor's Palace at Williamsburg is in the same style, and there are many similar examples in New England and Pennsylvania, notably at Philadelphia. Symmetry is a characteristic of all these buildings, which are substantially constructed. The interiors contain admirable woodwork and plasterwork, with a good deal of rich but refined decoration and panelling. Some of

the larger houses have subsidiary buildings as twin
pendants, entirely isolated, or connected with the main
block by curved or lateral colonnades in the Palladian
manner.

Surviving churches or 'meeting-houses' of the eighteenth century are still plentiful, and many are
picturesque if 'Protestant' in appearance. In New
England, the Congregational church with its classical
detail, its graceful white steeple, and its galleried
interior often occupies the place of honour on the village
green which would be filled by the Gothic parish-church
in rural England. There are good specimens in the 'Old
North' and 'Old South' Churches of Boston; at Dedham,
Dorchester, and Lenox, Mass.; and at Bennington,
Vermont. Most of them are built of wood, painted
white internally but with some use of mahogany by way
of contrast. More ambitious are the stately Christ
Church at Philadelphia (1727–37), St. Michael's at
Charleston in South Carolina (1751–60), and St. Paul's
in New York (1764–94). Gibbs was the English architect
followed by church-designers, and the principles laid
down by Wren for 'Protestant' places of worship were
generally accepted. Of public buildings erected during
the Georgian period, the Old State House at Boston
(1728) is the most venerable and interesting.

The influence of the Brothers Adam (p. 165) was at
least as potent in America as in England, and appears in
the delicate detail of many elegant houses in Boston and
elsewhere in the eastern states, especially in the work of
Samuel McIntire—a carpenter by training, of Charles
Bulfinch (1763–1844), and of Thomas Jefferson, an
amateur architect (1743–1826). Many of the larger
houses now became much more formal, and the idea

of circular, elliptical, and octagonal rooms was introduced as in England at the same period. Curved ('geometrical') staircases were also favoured, and Roman or Pompeian detail was used everywhere. The extraordinary career of Thomas Jefferson is without parallel in architectural history. A graduate of the College at Williamsburg, he passed out thence, before he was twenty, with a remarkable record in languages live and dead, mathematics and science. He was also an expert musician, dancer, sportsman, and horseman. Trained as a lawyer, he drafted the famous 'Declaration of Independence', became Governor of Virginia in 1779, and President of the United States in 1801, retiring eight years later to devote his remaining life to farming and building. Yet somehow he contrived, in his crowded career, to gain a considerable knowledge of architecture, prepared designs for a number of really important buildings, carried them out, and even submitted plans in competitions. Fig. 58 illustrates his own house at Monticello in Virginia and typifies his taste in design. In some ways, it recalls Lord Burlington's Villa at Chiswick (Fig. 46) in its Italian formality. He designed it when he was very young, in 1769, and supervised its erection over a long term of years: indeed, some say that he acted as his own contractor. There is no doubt that he acquired his knowledge of design out of books obtained from England and France, and from the study of classical monuments abroad. Monticello is a cheerful and comfortable dwelling in spite of its formal exterior. In American houses of this date, the columns are often much more slender than the rules of the 'Orders' prescribe.

There was nothing of the amateur about Bulfinch, who

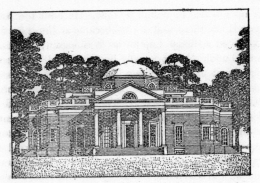

58. THOMAS JEFFERSON'S HOUSE (1769–1809) AT
MONTICELLO, VIRGINIA, U.S.A.

59. PRESBYTERIAN MEDICAL CENTER, NEW YORK:
PART OF FIRST INSTALMENT

set up practice in Boston in 1787. He built the New State House there, and in 1818 became architect for the unfinished national Capitol at Washington; but that noble building had originally been designed by a complete amateur, Dr. William Thornton, who had been selected for the task by no less a person than George Washington himself in 1793. The dome, constructed of iron, is an imposing addition of the mid-nineteenth century. The other celebrated building in Washington, commonly called 'The White House', was erected in 1792–9 by an Irish architect from Dublin, named James Hoban, and is an admirable design showing some French influence. The City Hall of New York (1803–12) is a splendid monument of the same period. The first building in America which completely accepted the Greek Revival is the Thaddeus Burr House at Fairfield, Conn. (1790).

Hitherto, all external influences mentioned here as affecting American architecture of the eighteenth century have been English; but we must not overlook two other sources. The Spanish 'missions' on the Californian coast present a sharp contrast with anything emanating from London or Paris or Italy, and are exotic, picturesque, and very rustic: they were built between 1769 and 1825. Compared with the prim meeting-houses of New England, they are full of colour, and they appear far older than they really are. An American architect has written that they have produced in modern times 'perhaps the loveliest daughter of our architecture—a daughter with the vigorous constitution of the north and the slumberous eyes and orchid colouring of old Mexico'. Traces of Spanish Baroque influence are also evident in New Orleans, where the Spaniards were in possession from 1769 to 1799, but there the prevailing atmosphere of the old quarter is French, especially in the Convent of the Ursulines (1730-4). In Québec and Montréal, too, there are many buildings entirely French in character, even later than the British conquest in 1763.

Washington was laid out on virgin soil in 1792 by a Frenchman, Major L'Enfant, and may be considered the most magnificent city plan in the world, a wonderful combination of artistic vision with monumental splendour and practical sense. The impression produced on my own mind by the splendid display of large perspectives and plans of Washington, exhibited at the First Town Planning Conference in London in 1910, remains still vivid.

The period 1820-1900 in America witnessed the same dreary succession of revivals as in England (described in Chapter 12), but with a few incidental variations. For the first forty years of this period, up to the Civil War of 1861-5, the Greek Revival had a tremendous vogue in the States, and travelled rapidly westwards with the settlers' wagons. Greek or Graeco-Roman buildings erected between 1830 and 1860 included Girard College at Philadelphia (1833-7), innumerable dwelling-houses, churches of all denominations, even synagogues, the Treasury Building at Washington (1836), several custom-houses, and some state capitols. Trinity Church in New York (1846) is a rare and outstanding example of neo-Gothic a generation ahead of the fashion. St. Patrick's Cathedral, also in New York (1858), is another early specimen of revived Gothic, but the full blast of that movement did not affect America till 1865 or so, when secular buildings began to be designed in a form which includes a good deal of Venetian detail, and therefore suggests that Ruskin is to blame for its popularity in America, as in England. A typical example of this Ruskinian Gothic is the Old Art Museum at Boston (1872–5). Only a few years later, America produced a fleeting but distinctive phase which has come to be called the 'Romanesque Revival'. Its chief exponent was H. H. Richardson, who practised for twenty years (1866–86) and during that time left his mark for all to see. His masterpiece is considered to be Trinity Church at Boston (1877), certainly a competent piece of grouping and a pleasant change from orthodox Gothic, but not unlike Union Church at Islington in London, built in 1876. Richardson had studied for many years at the École des Beaux Arts in Paris, but did not, like many of his contemporaries, attempt to popularize French architecture of the Haussmann type in his own land, where it had a brief spell of favour. At the World's Fair at Chicago in 1893, Louis Sullivan, another pioneer, designed the striking Transportation Building, in which he endeavoured to avoid all traditional forms of architectural expression and to create a new and distinctively American style. Domestic architecture was, for the most part, at a low ebb during the third quarter of the nineteenth century, and suffered from at least as many defects as its counterpart in England (p. 182), but had greatly improved before America entered the first world-war in 1917.

The three types of building in which America has made her most distinctive contribution to modern architecture do not include houses or churches, but comprise collegiate buildings in some form of English late Gothic or Tudor, public buildings of revived classic design, and, of course, 'skyscrapers'. For America, the

Gothic Revival has never died for academic buildings, where the compelling charm of the two old English universities has perpetuated the tradition of the sixteenth century in spite of all modern influences. The lavish generosity of wealthy benefactors, coupled with the abundance of illustrated folios describing Gothic architecture, compiled by American as well as English architects, has produced a great number of large institutions, each grouped round a spacious campus; they may be regrettable anachronisms but they have an undeniable attraction. The most distinguished firm of practitioners in the neo-Gothic field were Cram, Goodhue and Ferguson, whose work was done between 1895 and 1914; but they are best known for their splendid churches, notably St. Thomas's in New York City (1906).

Among designers of public buildings in the classical style, the palm must be awarded to the two firms of McKim, Mead and White and of Carrère and Hastings, both products of the French Beaux Arts system. The former firm were responsible for the Boston Public Library (1887–95), the buildings of Columbia University (1893) and the Pennsylvania Station at New York (1906–10); the latter for the New York Public Library (1897–1910). These few examples are selected from a host of others as typical of the high standard achieved in the monumental field.

Skyscrapers, so distinctive of the modern United States, are now also found in Canada and many other parts of the world, but had their origin as long ago as 1887, when the first multi-storey skeleton structure in iron, the Tacoma Building, was erected in Chicago, a mere thirteen storeys above ground. The subsequent evolution of this type, with the various attempts by architects to clothe it in 'period' masonry—at first classic; then, as at the Woolworth Building in New York (1911–13), Gothic—cannot be traced here; but Fig. 59 shows the most recent phase of design, where no effort is made to apply traditional ornamental features to its stark exterior, and relief is obtained by recessing the higher storeys in order to provide light and air, as was done at the Senate House of London University (Fig. 55). Whatever critics may say of the staccato majesty of the New York sky-line, where a rock foundation permits of almost unlimited vertical expansion, the skyscraper is a rather vulgar work of architecture, apt to be admired— like the Pyramids—merely for its size, regardless of the fact that it dwarfs its neighbours and surroundings in a most overbearing manner and causes insoluble traffic problems at its feet.

Between the two great wars, architectural thought in America was dominated by the wayward genius of Frank Lloyd Wright, but it remains to be seen whether his efforts to popularize international *modernismus* will permanently influence the curiously traditional tastes of our Transatlantic cousins, or whether the 'angry obscurities'—to quote a recent English critic—of his polemical writings will effect a conversion. In America, as in England, architecture seems destined to undergo another upheaval during the next few years, but the nature of that change is unpredictable.

BIBLIOGRAPHY

I. GENERAL

ADDY, S. O. *The Evolution of the English House*
ATKINSON, T. D. *A Glossary of English Architecture*
BRADDELL, DARCY. *How to Look at Buildings*
BRAUN, H. *The Story of the English House*
BRIGGS, M. S. *The Architect in History*
BUTLER, A. S. G. *The Substance of Architecture*
CHOISY, A. *Histoire de l'Architecture* (2 vols.)
FLETCHER, SIR B. F. *A History of Architecture on the Comparative Method*
GOTCH, J. A. *The Growth of the English House*
HAMMERTON, J. A. (ed.) *Wonders of the Past* (3 vols.)
JACKSON, SIR T. G. *Architecture*
LETHABY, W. R. *Form in Civilization* [essays]
MARCH PHILLIPPS, L. *The Works of Man* [essays]
QUENNELL, M. & C. H. B. *A History of Everyday Things in England*
ROBERTSON, H. M. *Architecture Explained*
RUSKIN, JOHN. *The Seven Lamps of Architecture*
SIMPSON, F. M. *A History of Architectural Development* (3 vols.)
STATHAM, H. H. *A Short Critical History of Architecture*
TALLMADGE, T. E. [American] *The Story of England's Architecture*

II. THE BEGINNINGS

BELL, E. *Architecture of Ancient Egypt*
        Pre-Hellenic Architecture in the Ægean
        Early Architecture in Western Asia
CAPART, J. *Egyptian Art*
CHOISY, A. *L'art de bâtir chez les Egyptiens*
PETRIE, SIR W. M. F. *Egyptian Architecture*

III. THE GREEKS

ANDERSON, SPIERS, & DINSMOOR. *Architecture of Ancient Greece*

BELL, E. *Hellenic Architecture*

FYFE, D. T. *Hellenistic Architecture*

LIVINGSTONE, SIR R. (ed.) *The Legacy of Greece*

ROBERTSON, D. S. *Handbook of Greek and Roman Architecture*

IV. THE ROMANS

ANDERSON, SPIERS, & ASHBY. *Architecture of Ancient Rome*

BAILEY, C. (ed.). *The Legacy of Rome*

CHOISY, A. *L'art de bâtir chez les Romains*

RIVOIRA, G. T. *Roman Architecture*

ROBERTSON, D. S. *Handbook of Greek and Roman Architecture*

VITRUVIUS. *De Architectura* (trans. F. Granger, 2 vols.)

V. THE DARK AGES

ARNOLD & GUILLAUME (eds.) *The Legacy of Islam*

BRIGGS, M. S. *Muhammadan Architecture in Egypt and Palestine*

CLAPHAM, A. W. *Romanesque Architecture in Western Europe*
    English Romanesque Architecture before the Conquest

HAMILTON, J. A. *Byzantine Architecture*

JACKSON, SIR T. G. *Byzantine and Romanesque Architecture* (2 vols.)

LETHABY, W. R. *Medieval Art*

RIVOIRA, G. T. *Lombardic Architecture* (2 vols.)

VI. THE NORMANS

CLAPHAM, A. W. *English Romanesque Architecture after the Conquest*

—also the works of Jackson and Rivoira cited under V

VII–VIII. *GOTHIC IN ENGLAND*

BOND, F. *Gothic Architecture in England*
   English Church Architecture (2 vols.)
GODFREY, W. H. *Story of Architecture in England*, Vol. I
JACKSON, SIR T. G. *Gothic Architecture* (2 vols.)
LETHABY, W. R. *Medieval Art*
POWER, C. E. *English Medieval Architecture* (3 vols.)
PRIOR, E. S. *English Medieval Art*
   A History of Gothic Architecture in England
THOMPSON, A. H. *Cathedral Churches of England*
WEST, G. H. *Gothic Architecture in England and France*

IX. *EARLY RENAISSANCE IN ENGLAND*

BLOMFIELD, SIR R. *History of Renaissance Architecture in
         England* (2 vols.)
      *Short History of Renaissance Architecture
         in England*
GOTCH, J. A. *Early Renaissance Architecture in England*
GOTCH & BROWN. *Architecture of the Renaissance in England*
   (2 vols.)
JACKSON, SIR T. G. *The Renaissance of Roman Architecture:*
   Vol. II., *England*
SCOTT, GEOFFREY. *The Architecture of Humanism*
SITWELL, S. *British Architects and Craftsmen:* 1600–1830

X. *INIGO JONES & CHRISTOPHER WREN*

BELCHER & MACARTNEY. *Later Renaissance Architecture in
   England* (2 vols.)
BIRCH, G. H. *London Churches of the 17th and 18th centuries*
GOTCH, J. A. *Inigo Jones*
MILMAN, L. *Sir Christopher Wren*
WEAVER, SIR L. *Sir Christopher Wren*
WEBB, G. *Wren*
   —also works of Blomfield, Jackson, & Sitwell cited
   under IX above and publications (20 vols.) of the
   Wren Society.

XI. LATE RENAISSANCE IN ENGLAND

BOLTON, A. T. *Architecture of Robert and James Adam*
                    The Portrait of Sir John Soane
BRIGGS, M. S. *Baroque Architecture*
RICHARDSON, A. E. *Monumental Classic Architecture in the 17th and 18th centuries*
SUMMERSON, J. N. *Georgian London*
WHISTLER, L. *Sir John Vanbrugh*
—also works of Belcher & Macartney, Blomfield, Jackson, & Sitwell cited under X above.

XII. 'THE BATTLE OF THE STYLES'

BLOMFIELD, SIR R. *Norman Shaw*
CLARK, SIR K. *The Gothic Revival*
JACKSON, HOLBROOK. *William Morris*
LETHABY, W. R. *Philip Webb*
SCOTT, SIR GILBERT. *Recollections*
SUMMERSON, J. N. *John Nash*

XIII. THE TWENTIETH CENTURY IN ENGLAND

ABERCROMBIE, SIR P. (ed.) *The Book of the Modern House*
BLOMFIELD, SIR R. *Modernismus*
BRIGGS, M. S. *Building To-day*
HOWARD, EBENEZER. *Garden Cities of Tomorrow*
MARRIOTT, C. *Modern English Architecture*
REILLY, SIR C. H. *Representative British Architects*
YORKE & PENN. *A Key to Modern Architecture*

XIV. ARCHITECTURE IN AMERICA

BRIGGS, M. S. *The Homes of the Pilgrim Fathers*
CHANDLER, J. E. *The Colonial House*
KELLY, J. F. *Early Domestic Architecture of Connecticut*
KIMBALL, FISKE. *Domestic Architecture of the American Colonies . . . etc.*
TALLMADGE, T. E. *The Story of Architecture in America*

INDEX

All buildings are indexed according to locality: e.g. 'Crystal Palace' appears under 'London', and 'Theatre of Marcellus' under 'Rome'.

Aachen Cathedral, 59
Abbeville, 108
Abercorn, Saxon cross at, 63
Abingdon, church at, 61
Abydos, temple at, 11
Adam, R., 164, 165-6, 207
Agrigentum, temples at, 27
Alatri, temple at, 34
Alexander the Great, 11, 30
Alexandria, 30, 56, 63
Allen, R., 165
Amiens Cathedral, 91
Ancona, arch at, 44
Archer, T., 168
Arles, amphitheatre at, 44
Ashbridge Park, 175
Aston Hall, 129-31, 134; Fig. 33
Athelhampton Hall, 129, 134
Athens, 18-31
  Acropolis, 29
  Erechtheion, 28
  Houses in, 30
  Monument of Lysikrates, 29; Fig. 7
  Olympeion, 20
  Parthenon, 20, 22-3, 25, 27
  Propylaea, 29
  Temple on the Ilissos, 20, 28
  Temple of Niké Apteros, 28
  'Theseion', 20, 23, 25, 27; Figs. 5, 6
Audley End, 134

Augustine, St., 49, 60, 62
Augustus, emperor, 32, 34, 35, 38

Baalbek, 42, 43, 46
Babylon, 16
Bacon's Castle. *See* 'Virginia'
Bakewell, Saxon cross at, 63
Barfreston, church at, 74
Barnack, church at, 66
Barrington Court, 134
Barry, Sir C., 174, 176-7
Barton-on-Humber, church at, 66
Basevi, G., 173
Bath, Abbey (Cathedral), 81
  Circus, 165
  Crescent, 165
  Prior Park, 165
  Queen Square, 165
Bayeux Tapestry, the, 71
Beauvais Cathedral, 91
Becontree, 193
Belcher, J., 190
Benedict Biscop, 62
Benevento, arch at, 44
Bennington (Vermont), church, 207
Bentley, G. F., 192
Berlage, H. P., 194
Bernay, church at, 70
Bernini, G. L., 149
Bethlehem, church at, 52
Beverley Minster, 108, 112

Bewcastle, Saxon cross at, 63
Bexhill, Pavilion at, 196
Bexley Heath, 'Red House', 184
Bibury, cottages at, 135; Fig. 35
Birmingham, Town Hall, 42
    Cathedral, 168
    University, 190
Bishopstoke, church at, 66
Blandford, church at, 168
Blenheim Palace, 159–61
Blickling Hall, 134
Bodiam Castle, 115
Bodley, G. F., 181, 192
Bolsover Castle, 134
Boston (Mass.), Revere House, 204
    churches at, 207
    New State House, 210
    Old Art Museum, 212
    Old State House, 207
    Public Library, 213
    Trinity Church, 212
Boston 'Stump', 176
Bourges Cathedral, 91
Bournville, 188–9
Bradbourne, Saxon Cross, 63
Bradford-on-Avon, church at, 64; Fig. 18
Brading, villa at, 46
Bradwell, church at, 60
Bramshill House, 134
Breamore, church at, 66
Brighton, 172
    Pavilion, 167, 170
Bristol, chapel at, 168
Brixworth, church at, 61, 68
Brodrick, C., 174
Brunelleschi, F., 125, 143
Buildwas Abbey, 88
Bulfinch, C., 207, 208, 210
Burghley House, 134
Burlington, Lord, 163–4
Burton, D., 172

Bury St. Edmund's, Cathedral, 81
    chapel at, 155
Butterfield, W., 180
Buxton, Royal Crescent, 164
Byzantium, S. Irene, 55
    SS. Sergius and Bacchus, 55
    S. Sophia, 55

Caen, La Trinité, 72
    St. Étienne, 72
    St. Nicholas, 74
Caerleon, amphitheatre at, 44
Cairo, Mosque of Ibn Tūlūn, 58; Fig. 17
Caligula, emperor, 35
Cambridge, 116, 137, 157, 190
    Caius College, 137
    Downing College, 173
    Fitzwilliam Museum, 173
    Guildhall, 198
    King's College Chapel, 107, 110–11; Fig. 30
    Pembroke College, 149
    'Round Church', the, 81
    St. Benet, 66
    Senate House, 163
    Trinity College, 150
Campbell, C., 163
Canterbury, Cathedral, 72, 79, 81, 88, 112
    early churches at, 60, 61, 72
Cardiff, civic buildings, 191
Carlisle Cathedral, 81
'Carr of York', 164
Carrère and Hastings, 213
Castle Howard, 153, 159–60
Caudebec, 108
Cerisy-la-Forêt, abbey of, 74
Chambers, Sir W., 166
Chantilly, stables at, 160

Charlemagne, 59
Charleston (U.S.A.), church at, 207
Chartres Cathedral, 91, 105
Chastleton House, 134
Chaucer, G., 118
Chedworth, villa at, 46
Cheltenham, 173
Chequers Court, 137; Fig. 39
Chester Cathedral, 81
Chichester Cathedral, 72
Chicago, World's Fair, 212
　Tacoma Building, 213
Chippendale, T., 166
Chiswick House, 164; Fig. 46
Chorley Wood, house at, 185–6; Fig. 53
Chysauster, 8
Cockerell, C. R., 173
Coggeshall, 'Paycockes', 116
Colchester, temple at, 42
　Town Hall, 190
Collcutt, T. E., 190
Constantine, emperor, 35, 48, 49
Constantinople. See 'Byzantium'
Cooper, Sir E., 191
Corbridge, church at, 62
'Corbusier, Le', 194–5
Cordova, Great Mosque, 58
Cori, temple at, 40
Corinth, temples at, 18, 27
Cothay House, 116
Cowes, 'castle' at, 172
Cram, Goodhue and Ferguson, 213
Crete, 16–17, 19, 22
Croft, Saxon cross at, 63
Cromwell, Oliver, 124
　Thomas, 124, 141
Croydon, Whitgift Hospital, 139
Croyland Abbey, 105

Damascus, Great Mosque, 56
Dance, G., 163
Dartmoor, 8
Dawber, Sir E. G., 184, 186
Dedham (Mass.), church at, 207
Deerhurst, church at, 63
Delphi, temple at, 25
Dendera, temple at, 11
Dijon, 70
Diocletian, emperor, 35, 43, 44, 165
Domitian, emperor, 35
Dorchester (Mass.), church at, 207
Dudok, W. M., 194
Durham, Cathedral, 72 75, 78, 81
　Saxon cross, 63
Dymock, cottage at, Fig. 1, c.

Ealing, church at, 180
Earl's Barton, church at, 64–5; Fig. 19
Easby, Saxon cross at, 63
Edfu, temple at, 11
Edinburgh Cathedral, 180
Edward the Confessor, 70–1
Elmham, church at, 63
Ely Cathedral, 72, 81
Ephesus, temple at, 28
Escomb, church at, 62
Esna, temple at, 11
Eton College, 116
Evelyn, J., 148, 158
Exeter Cathedral, 78
Eyam, Saxon cross at, 63

Fairfield (Conn.), house at, 210
Farmington (Conn.), house at, 204
Fécamp, 70
Flitcroft, H., 163

Florence, 123
    Cathedral, 125
Folkestone, villa at, 46
Fonthill Abbey, 175
Fountains Abbey, 82, 88
    Hall, 134

George IV (Prince Regent),
    167, 170
George, Sir E., 184, 186
Germigny des Près, church
    at, 59
Gibbs, J., 157, 161-3, 167,
    206, 207
Giza, Pyramids of, 10
    Temple at, 10
Glasgow, churches in, 173
    University, 180
Glastonbury, 6, 63
    Abbot's Kitchen, 116
Gloucester Cathedral, 72, 75,
    81, 108
Great Chalfield Manor-
    house, 116
Great Exhibition (1851), 181
Great Paxton, church at, 66
Great Wakering, houses at,
    Fig. 38
Greenstead, church at, 66
Greenwich. See 'London'
Groombridge Place, 152,
    205; Fig. 42
Guildford, Abbot's Hospital,
    139
    Cathedral, 199
Guilford (Conn.), houses,
    204
Guiseley Rectory, 134; Fig.
    34

Haddon Hall, 115, 134
Hadrian, emperor, 35
Haifa, 196
Halifax, church at, 180
Hamburg, cathedral at, 177

Hampstead Garden Suburb,
    189
Hampton Court, 127, 146,
    150
Hardwick, P., 173
Hardwick Hall, 134
Hare, H. T., 190
Harewood, village of, 157
    House, 164
Harrow Weald, house at,
    192; Fig. 50
Hatfield House, 134
Hawksmoor, N., 159, 161,
    167
Hawton, church at, 108
Heckington, church at, 108
Hereford, 'Old House', 135;
    Fig. 36
Hertford, County Hall, 198
Hexham, crypt, 62
Hingham (Mass.), church at,
    204
Hoban, J., 210
Holkham Hall, 164
Horningsham, chapel at, 123
Hornsey, Town Hall, 197
Houghton Hall, 158, 163
Hovingham, Saxon cross at,
    63
Howard, E., 188-9, 192

Iffley, church at, 74, 75, 78;
    Fig. 20
Ilkley, church at, 182
Impington Village College,
    197
Inwood, H. W., 173
Ipswich, chapel at, 155
Iraq. See 'Mesopotamia'
Irton, Saxon cross at, 63
Isleworth, Syon House, 165

Jackson, Sir T. G., 190
Jarrow, church at, 62
Jefferson, T., 207, 208

Jerusalem, Church of Holy
    Sepulchre, 81
  'Dome of the Rock', 56
  Mosque of Aksa, 56
Jones, Inigo, 122, 134, 142-7
Jordans, 155
Julius Caesar, 34, 35
Jumièges Abbey, 70
Justinian, emperor, 55

Kahun, 12
Karnak, 10, 12; Fig. 3
Kedleston Hall, 165
Kenilworth Castle, 115
Kent, W., 163
Kenwood, 165
Kew, pagoda at, 166
Kilpeck, church at, 75; Fig.
    21
Kirby Hall, 134
Kirby Muxloe Castle, 116
Kirkstall Abbey, 82, 88
Klerk, L. de, 194
Knole Park, 134
Knossos, palace at, 16-17, 19
Knott, R., 191
Kom Ombo, temple at, 11

Lanchester and Richards,
    191, 198
Langley, B., 167
Laon Cathedral, 91
Lavenham, church at, 113
Leeds, St. John's church,
    147
  Town Hall, 174; Fig. 48
  University, 198
L'Enfant, Major, 211
Lenox (Mass.), church at,
    207
Leoni, G., 163
Lessay Abbey, 74
Letchworth, 188-9

Lincoln, Cathedral, 72, 78,
    88, 91, 94; Fig. 26A
  'The Jew's House', 82-3
Little Wenham Hall, 104
Liverpool, Cathedral, 191-2;
    Fig. 52
  St. George's Hall, 174
London, Adelphi, 165
  Albert Memorial, 178
  All Saints, Margaret Street,
    180
  All Souls', Langham Place,
    170
  Athenaeum Club, 28, 172,
    174; Fig. 47
  Bank of England, 43, 166
  Bridgewater House, 174
  British Museum, 173
  Buckingham Palace, 172
  Burlington House, 163
  Burlington School, 197
  Carlton House Terrace,
    170
  Central Hall, 191
  Charterhouse, hall, 139
  Chelsea Hospital, 150
  Chelsea, houses in, 197;
    Fig. 54
  City churches, 152, 155
  County Hall, 191
  Criminal Court, 190
  Crystal Palace, 181-2, 195
  Electra House, 190
  Euston Station, 27, 173
  Frognal, houses in, 197
  Government   Buildings,
    178, 191
  Gray's Inn Hall, 139
  Greenwich, Hospital, 146,
    150
  Greenwich,   Queen's
    House, 146-7; Fig. 40
  'Highpoint', 197
  Imperial College, 190
  Imperial Institute, 190

London :
  Holland House, 134
  Horse Guards, 164
  Houses of Parliament, 176-7
  Institute of Accountants, 190
  Kensington, church at, 180
  Kensington Palace, 150
  Lancaster House, 174
  Law Courts, 180
  Mansion House, 163
  Marble Arch, 44
  Masonic Hospital, 197
  Middle Temple Hall, 139
  National Gallery, 173
  Peckham Health Centre, 197
  Piccadilly Hotel, 182
  Port of London Building, 191
  Reform Club, 174
  Regent Street, 170, 172
  Regent's Park, 170
  St. Alban, Holborn, 180
  St. Dunstan-in-the-West, 176
  St. George, Bloomsbury, 167, 168
  St. James, Piccadilly, 155
  St. John, Westminster, 167
  St. Luke, Chelsea, 170
  St. Martin-in-the-Fields, 167, 168
  St. Mary Woolnoth, 167
  St. Mary-le-Strand, 167
  St. Pancras Church, 28, 173
  St. Pancras Station, 180
  St. Paul's Cathedral, 40, 149, 152-3; Figs. 43, 44
  St. Paul's, Covent Garden, 147
  Selfridge's Store, 190
  Soane Museum, 166

London :
  Somerset House, 166
  Southwark Cathedral, 81
  Stafford House, 174
  Staple Inn, 139
  Tower of, 76, 78
  Traveller's Club, 174
  Union Church, Islington, 212
  United Service Club, 170
  University, 198; Fig. 55
  University College, 173
  Victoria and Albert Museum, 164, 190
  War Office, 190
  Wesley's Chapel, 168
  Westminster Abbey, 70-1, 72, 91, 94, 107, 108, 126; Fig. 32
  Westminster Cathedral, 192
  Westminster Hall, 111, 177
  Whitehall, palace, 143-6; Fig. 41
Long Melford, church at, 113
Longleat, 123, 134
Lower Brockhampton, 116
Lutyens, Sir E. L., 184, 186
Lyminge, church at, 60

McKim, Mead, and White, 213
McIntire, S., 207
Mackintosh, C. R., 186
Maiden Castle, 8
Maisons, château of, 146, 149
Majano, G. da, 127
Manchester Town Hall, 180
Mansart, F., 149
Markenfield Hall, 104
Meare, 6
Michelangelo, 46
Miletus, temple at, 20, 28
Monkwearmouth, church at, 62

Montacute House, 134
Monticello (Va.), 208; Fig. 58
Montivilliers Abbey, 74
Montréal, McTavish House, 204
    Seminary, 205
Moor Park, 163
Moreton Old Hall, 134–5; Fig. 37
Morris, W., 181, 184
Mycenae, 17, 19

Nash, 'Beau', 165
Nash, John, 170, 172
Nero, emperor, 35
New Orleans, convent at, 211
New York, 201, 214
    City Hall, 210
    St. Patrick, 211
    St. Paul, 207
    Trinity Church, 211
    Public Library, 213
    Pennsylvania Station, 213
    St. Thomas, 213
    Columbia University, 213
    Woolworth Building, 214
    Medical Center, 214; Fig. 59
Newton, E., 186
Nîmes, Pont du Gard, 37; Fig. 9
    temple at, 37; Fig. 10
    amphitheatre at, 44
Nocera, Baptistery at, 53
Nonsuch Palace, 127
Northampton, the 'Round Church', 81
Norwich, Cathedral, 72, 78, 81, 87
    City Hall, 198
    'Old Meeting', 155

Oakham Castle, 104
Olympia, temples at, 18, 27

Orange, arch at, 44
    theatre of, 43
Osterley Park, 165
Ostia, houses at, 46; Fig. 14
Otley, Saxon cross at, 63
Oxburgh Hall, 116
Oxford, 115, 137, 142, 157, 190
    Ashmolean Museum, 173
    Cathedral, 81
    Christ Church, 150
    Keble College, 180
    Magdalen College Chapel, 112
    Municipal Buildings, 190
    Museum, 181; Fig. 49
    New College, 117
    Queen's College, 161; Fig. 45
    Radcliffe Library, 161
    Sheldonian Theatre, 149
    'Tower of the Five Orders', 42, 128, 137
    Wadham College, 137

Paestum, temple at, 25
Palladio, A., 125, 134, 145, 159, 163, 166, 206
Palmerston, Lord, 169, 178
Palmyra, 42, 46
Parenzo, basilica at, 50, 51; Fig. 16
Paris, Notre Dame, 91, 94, 105
Parker, B., 188–9
Pearson, J. L., 181
Peiraeus, the, 31
Penshurst Place, 115; Fig. 31
Pericles, 30–1
Perugia, arch at, 34
Peterborough Cathedral, 63, 76, 79, 81, 105
Philadelphia   (U. S. A.), churches at, 204
    Girard College, 211

Philae, temple at, 11
Pompeii, 46
Port Sunlight, 188–9
Praeneste, 35
Prague, Cathedral, 89
    Synagogue, 104
Priene, temple at, 28
Pugin, A. (the elder), 175
    A. W. N., 177
Pyramids of Egypt, 10–11

Québec, convent at, 204

Ravenna, churches at, 51, 55
    Baptistery at, 53
Reculver, church at, 60–1
Reims Cathedral, 91, 105
Repton, crypt at, 66
Richard of Gainsborough, 105
Richardson, H. H., 212
Rickman, T., 87–8, 175
Ripon, crypt at, 62
Rochester, Cathedral, 81
    St. Andrew's, 60
Rome, 32–47
    Arch of Constantine, 44; Fig. 13
    Arch of Septimius Severus, 44
    Arch of Titus, 44
    Baptistery of Constantine, 53
    Basilica Julia, 35
    Basilica of Constantine, 38
    Baths of Caracalla, 44
    Baths of Diocletian, 38, 44–5; Fig. 12
    Catacombs, 50
    Cloaca Maxima, 33
    Colosseum, 40, 44
    Houses in, 46
    Imperial Palaces, 35
    Mausoleum of Augustus, 35

Rome:
    Pantheon, 38, 43; Fig. 11
    S. Agnese, 51
    S. Clemente, 51
    S. Costanza, 53
    S. Giovanni in Laterano, 51
    S. Lorenzo, 51
    S. Maria Maggiore, 51
    S. Paolo, 51
    St. Peter's, 51
    S. Sabina, 51, 52–3; Fig. 15
    S. Stefano Rotondo, 53
    Temple of Fortuna Virilis, 40
    Temple of Jupiter, 35, 42
    Temple of Mars Ultor, 42
    Temple of Venus and Rome, 42
    Temple of Vesta, 43
    Theatre of Marcellus, 43, 149
Rouen, 68, 108, 177
Ruskin, J., 1, 4, 89, 180, 181, 184, 191
Ruthwell, Saxon cross at, 63

St. Albans Cathedral, 72, 78, 79, 81, 104
St. Denis Cathedral, 88
St. Leonards-on-Sea, 172
Salem (Mass.), 202
    John Ward House, 202; Fig. 56
    Hathaway House, 204
    'Seven Gables', 204
Salisbury Cathedral, 89, 91, 94, 96–9, 111; Figs. 24, 25
Salonica, St. Sophia, 55
Sandbach, Saxon cross at, 63
Sargon, King, 15
Saugus (Mass.), house at, 204

Scott, Sir Gilbert, 2, 169, 177–8, 180
Scott, Sir Giles, 192
Scott, Sir Walter, 175
Scrivelsby, 'Teapot Hall', 6; Fig. 1B
Segesta, temples at, 27
Segovia, aqueduct at, 37
Selinus, temples at, 18, 20, 27
Senlis Cathedral, 88
Sens Cathedral, 88
Shaw, Norman, 182, 184
Sherborne Abbey, 112
Shute, J., 125
Silchester, 49, 59–60
Simons, R., 139
Sizergh Castle, 134
Skara Brae, 8
Smirke, Sir R., 173
Smithson, R., 139
Soane, Sir J., 43, 166
Sompting, church at, 66
Southwark. See 'London'
Southwell Cathedral, 78, 79, 103; Fig. 26B
South Wingfield Manor-house, 116
Spalato, Palace at, 43, 165
Speke Hall, 134
Stanton Harcourt, 116
Stapleford, Saxon cross at, 63
Stokesay Castle, 104, 115; Fig. 30
Stonehenge, 8
Strawberry Hill, 167, 170
Street, G. E., 180
Sulla, 35
Sullivan, L., 212
Sutton Place, 129
Swansea, Civic Centre, 198
Syracuse, temples at, 27

Tattershall Castle, 116
'Teapot Hall.' See 'Scrivelsby'

Tel Aviv, 196
Temple Newsam, 134
Tewkesbury Abbey, 72, 78
Thebes (Egypt), temples at, 10, 14, 22; Figs. 3, 4
Theodore of Tarsus, 62
Thomson ('Greek'), A., 173
Thornton, Dr. W., 210
Thorpe, J., 139
Timgad, 46
Tiryns, 17, 19
Titus, emperor, 35
Tivoli, temple at, 43
Topsfield (Mass.), house at, 204
Torcello Cathedral, 51
Torrigiano, 126–7
Trajan, emperor, 35
Truro Cathedral, 181; Fig. 51

Unwin, Sir R., 188–9, 192
Ur, 15–16

Vanbrugh, Sir J., 159–61
Venice, St. Mark's, 55
Verona, amphitheatre at, 44
Versailles, palace at, 150
Verulamium, theatre at, 43
Vicenza, 145
  Villa Capra, near, 164
Virginia, Bacon's Castle, 202
  St. Luke's Church, 201–2
Vitruvius, 26, 27, 28, 40, 125, 126, 145
Voysey, C. F. A., 181, 185–6
Vredeman de Vries, 127

Walpole, H., 142, 158, 167, 170
Walpole, chapel at, 147
Warkworth Castle, 116
Warwick, Beauchamp Chapel, 112
  St. Mary's, 147
Washington, G., 210

Washington, Capitol, 210
    Plan of, 211
    Treasury, 211
    'White House', 210
Waterhouse, A., 180
Webb, Sir A., 190
Webb, John, 146
Webb, Philip, 184
Wells Cathedral, 91, 104–5
Welwyn Garden City, 188–9,
    193
Wentworth Woodhouse, 163
Wesley, J., 168
Westminster. *See* 'London'
'Westover', Virginia, 206;
    Fig. 57
Weymouth, 172
Wilkins, W., 173
William of Sens, 88
William de Wermington, 105
Williamsburg (Va.), 205–6
Winchelsea Church, Fig. 27
Winchester Cathedral, 72,
    81, 112
    College, 116, 117
    St. Peter's Chapel, 170

Windsor, St. George's Chapel,
    107, 110
Wing, church at, 63
Wollaton Hall, 127–8, 139
Wolsey, Cardinal, 127
Wood, J. ('of Bath'), 164–5
Woodham Walter, church at,
    202
Worcester Cathedral, 72, 81,
    94
Worksop Priory, 78
Worth, church at, 64
Wren, Sir C., 107, 122, 141,
    142, 148–55, 156, 161,
    168, 205, 206
Wright, F. L., 214
Wyatt, J., 175
Wycliffe, J., 107
Wykeham, William of, 117

York Minster, 79, 91, 100,
    112

Zennor, 8

Printed by Butler & Tanner Ltd., Frome and London